The OCR Student's Guide

by Tony Parkinson and Roy Blatchford

To be used alongside
The OCR Poetry Anthology
and The OCR Teacher's Pack

APPROVED BY
THE OCR CHIEF
EXAMINERS

English 1500
English Literature 1501

Step-by-step to a better grade!

CONTENTS

Step-by-step to a better grade	3
Your checklist for the English and English Literature exams	4
Your quick guide to the English and English Literature exams	5

1 THE OCR NON-FICTION AND MEDIA TEXTS PAPER — 6
What the exam requires — 6
An example of pre-released material — 7
How to make a summary – in six steps — 8
How to comment on content and style – in six steps — 14
How to write an argument — 21

2 THE OCR LITERARY TEXTS PAPER — 24
What the exam requires: other cultures — 24
Stories from other cultures – in six steps — 25
How to get a better grade for the two writing questions — 34

3 COURSEWORK: ENGLISH — 38
A useful checklist — 38
Your quick guide to the OCR English and English Literature coursework — 39
Writing for different purposes — 40
Drafting and redrafting — 42
Word processing — 43
How writers use language: useful tips — 44

4 COURSEWORK : ENGLISH LITERATURE — 46
What the exam requires — 46
Literary tradition — 47

5 HOW TO TACKLE ENGLISH LITERATURE EXAM QUESTIONS — 48
Poetry: how to make comparisons – in six steps — 48
Extracts: how to tackle questions – in six steps — 52

6 GENERAL REVISION — 58
Tips to improve your reading — 58
Tips to improve your speaking and listening — 59
Tips to improve your writing — 60

7 THE OCR EXAM! — 62
Revision – the night before — 62
The day itself – five steps to a better grade — 63
Index — 64

Step-by-step to a better grade

Dear Student,

This guide will inform you about what you need to do for your OCR English and English Literature examinations. It gives you advice, tips and practice to help you achieve the very best grade.

It has been approved by the OCR Chief Examiners.

You are the most important influence on your result. Make sure you get enough practice. The more you practise the better your **writing**, your **reading** and your **speaking** and **listening** will be ... and the better your grade will be!

Ask yourself:

▶ How can I improve my **writing**?

▶ How good is my **reading**?

▶ Am I a good communicator when **speaking and listening**?

This guide shows you the different types of question you will have to do in the examination.

To help you with these, the book takes the following steps:

STEP 6 Tips for revision

STEP 5 Practise for a better grade

STEP 4 More helpful details for you to remember

STEP 3 Notes or sample answers

STEP 2 How to answer the question

STEP 1 Look closely at the question

Remember to show this guide to your family. They will want to know what you are doing and offer you extra help.

Good luck, study hard and use this guide to help you improve your grade!

Tony Parkinson   **Roy Blatchford**

The English and English Literature exams

Your checklist for the English and English Literature exams

English

Non-fiction and media texts

Before the exam	A sheet of ideas to give you the topic.
In the exam paper	Two extracts to read, each with a question to test your reading. One piece of writing to argue a point of view.

Literary Texts

Before the exam	A story from another culture to prepare.
In the exam paper	One question based on the story. Two pieces marked for writing.

Your teacher may give marks for your **speaking and listening** in any English lesson – make sure you know when!

Your folder will normally have five or six pieces of work. The first two are for English (and are marked for writing skills). Any of the pieces about what you have read (except texts by writers from other countries) may be used for English and English Literature coursework.

You can take your set books into the exam to help you check facts and quotations. You may write in your books – but not long notes or essay plans.

English Literature

You must study six books, three for the exam paper and three for the coursework. The books studied for English Literature coursework must be different from those for the exam.

Checklist

Write here the names of the books you are using for **coursework**:

1. _____

2. _____

3. _____

Your quick guide to the English and English Literature exams

 This is the name of your English/English Literature Examining Group. You need to know it when you fill in forms for work or for colleges and universities.

English: what you have to do

Exam paper: Non-fiction and media texts
Three questions   2 hours + 10 minutes reading time  30%

Exam paper: Literary texts
Three questions   2 hours + 10 minutes reading time  30%

Coursework: Speaking and listening
Three activities (marked by your teacher during the course)  20%

Coursework: Reading and writing
Two pieces of writing, and
Three responses to what you have read
- a Shakespeare play
- a novel or short story/ies
- poetry
 20%

Total = 100%

English Literature: what you have to do

Set books paper
Three questions, each on a different book $2\frac{1}{2}$ hours  70%

Coursework
Three responses to books you have studied
This coursework may be the same as your responses to reading for English Coursework: ask your teacher about this.
- drama
- a novel or short story/ies
- poetry
 30%

Total = 100%

Checklist

Ask your teacher what your set books are for the English Literature examination paper and write them here:

1
2
3

1 THE OCR NON-FICTION AND MEDIA TEXTS PAPER

What the exam requires

Read	Write
A non-fiction text*	Q1 Select and summarise.
A media text*	Q2 Comment on content and style.
	Q3 Q4 A choice of two titles for writing, in which you discuss, argue or persuade. The subjects are related to the topic of the paper (which you know in advance).

*The two texts can be in either order. The questions are in the order shown above.

About twelve weeks before the exam, OCR sends you a sheet of **pre-released material**. It gives you ideas which are useful when you do Q3 or Q4. On page 7 you can see what this sheet might look like.

What is a non-fiction text?

Non-fiction can be for:

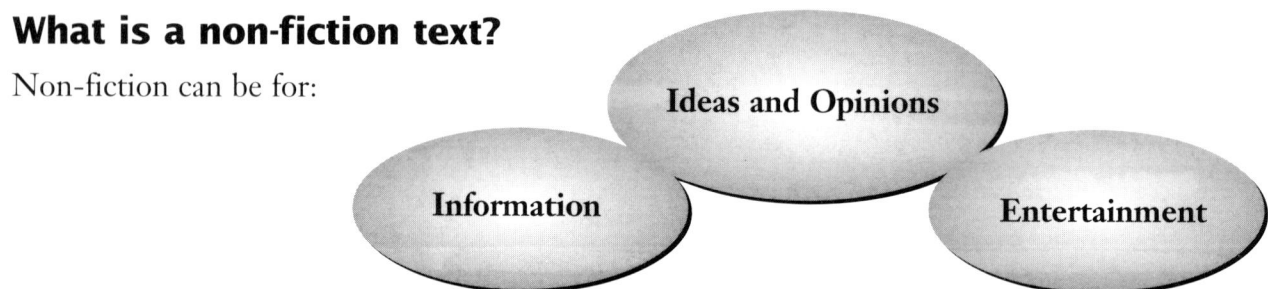

From encyclopaedias, text books, magazines, autobiographies, biographies, journals, diaries, travel literature, letters and leaflets.

What is a media text?

▶ Media texts are from newspapers (reports, articles, features, editorials), magazines, pamphlets, charity appeals, personalised letters, travel brochures or advertisements.

▶ Most media texts try to **persuade** you, for example to spend your money on their product, or to agree with their **propaganda**. Newspapers want you to agree with their views and to think that they are leaders in morality, style and culture. You need to think about the techniques media texts use.

▶ The text is often in its original layout with pictures and graphics. Whenever this happens, you may comment on any feature of the text – not just the words.

An example of pre-released material

Topic: Good and bad neighbours and how to deal with them

Legal Wrangles

Disputes between neighbours, writes our legal expert, can last years and cost thousands. Neighbours argue over boundaries involving a few centimetres. In other cases over-hanging trees can cause years of hatred.

Politician Urges Good Neighbourliness

A local MP addressed a packed meeting on Monday. Hundreds flocked to the Town Hall after *The Star* reported a case of child neglect. They were told that good neighbourliness could prevent similar cases. Families spent too much time watching TV and did not even know the family next door.

Visit

An occasional visit to an elderly person, or looking after someone's children could make all the difference. If we were more aware, we might notice that the child next door was underfed and unhappy.

Neighbourhood Watch Sparks Snooper Protest

Walnut Close was proud of its Neighbourhood Watch scheme – net curtains twitched, numberplates were checked and salesmen scrutinised. But faces were red when Grandad Jolly visited his grandchildren at number 20. 'I'd come to babysit,' he said. 'I answered the door and there were two policewomen, a constable and a lot of blue lights.' A police spokesperson said despite the embarrassment, it was better to be safe than sorry.

Teenage Terror Turns Over New Leaf

17-year-old Aileen Jones was presented with the Junior Good Citizen award yesterday for her work with elderly residents in Old Town. She and her friends have been shopping, gardening and cleaning homes. The verdict? 'She's a wonder.' But Aileen's proud mother remembers her daughter as a tearaway. 'She was dreadful,' she said, 'always in trouble up and down the street.'

DIY Neighbour From Hell

Fred Gainsmith is London's busiest DIY man. Every day and night he saws, hammers and drills inside and out. He boasts: 'My home is the best improved anywhere. I love knocking things down and building bits on.'

Bathroom Collapse

His neighbour thinks otherwise. While washing her hands she heard an 'almighty bang' and the taps fell off the wall. Then Fred's grinning face appeared through a gaping hole. 'It didn't amuse me,' said Mrs Green. Fred is unrepentant: 'A bit of give and take is needed. We're British.'

Activity

Make a list of the five sub-topics suggested by these news items and make rough notes of your ideas (e.g. advantages of Neighbourhood Watch).

How to make a summary – in six steps

Read this passage and then follow Steps *1* to *3* to a better grade.

Enter Pan with a crash of bells

Nigel Howard *joins the ancient and ear-shattering ritual which signals the start of Lent on the Aegean island of Skyros*

The butcher's boy was working hard, delivering meat by wheelbarrow all afternoon to the tavernas on the steep main street of Skyros town. Each wheelbarrow trip was loaded with a single goat's carcass almost as long as the boy was tall.

Business was brisk at the butcher's as it was carnival and because it was the last weekend before the meat-free period of Lent began. Standing in the main square in the early spring sunshine we watched the butcher's boy and his barrow clatter and bounce down the cobbled street. The square was filled with people. The boy increased his pace. He knew the *geri* would come soon and he did not want to miss anything.

Skyros town, on the northeast side of Skyros island – one of the Sporades in the northern Aegean – is small, picturesque and, normally, quiet. Its narrow, twisting streets wind up towards the hilltop monastery of St George. The main square in front of the town hall is normally empty except towards evening when elderly couples stroll out to watch the sun set behind the stony mountains to the west. But this afternoon was different.

The air was full of the snarl and stink of two-stroke engines as farmers and their families arrived perched aboard three-wheeler goods vehicles – the standard mode of transport in rural Greece. Mercedes taxis hurried well-dressed Athenians in from the ferry port, hooting their way past old men on donkeys and boys on bicycles. Tented cafes and restaurants now lined the square where friends and families strolled and chatted and everywhere colourfully dressed toddlers waved tiny blue-and-white Greek flags.

Gradually, as blue dusk began to fill the square, the crowd fell silent. Then the sound began. At first it was a rhythmic crunch, like heavy surf on a far-away pebble beach, but as it grew nearer and louder different notes could be distinguished. Slowly the noise increased and soon the whole town seemed to be pounding. In the square, hundreds of faces turned westwards and from the far side came a cry: 'The *geri*, the *geri*.' And with a thundering crash of sound the ancient Greek god Pan danced out of the sunset.

The creature was nearly two metres tall and dressed in a black shaggy hooded coat. Beneath the hood its face was covered by a dangling mask made from the whole skin of a baby goat. It wore heavy white woollen shepherd's trousers and traditional Skyrian leather sandals. Around its waist hung more than 20 heavy bronze goat bells.

The half-man, half-goat danced forward through the crowd. Other similar creatures appeared from different directions, and with a clashing of bells they danced ponderously towards each other, meeting in the middle of the square. There they formed a circle and, leaning on their crooks, they stood, hips swaying and bells clanging.

These were the legendary *geri*, the goat dancers of Skyros. Every year, on the two Sundays before Lent, they perform their strange pagan dance. Boys practise for the dance almost from the time they take their first steps. To be a *geros*, as the individual dancer is known, is considered an honour.

Today Skyros is famous for its goats, goat produce, goat dancers and its beautifully crafted miniature furniture which is still regarded as a valuable addition to any Greek girl's wedding dowry.

How to make a summary – in six steps

STEP 1 — Look closely at this question

Question: *Summarise the sights and sounds of Skyros on a normal day and contrast them with those of carnival day when the geri dance.*

- Look in the passage on page 8 for references to **sights** (things you see) and **sounds** (things you hear) on a normal (ordinary) day.
- Look for (**contrasts**) differences on carnival day.

Highlight **sights**, **sounds**, **contrast**.

STEP 2 — How to answer the question

- Use only **relevant** details.
- Expect many points – maybe 20 – so search for them.
- Make rough notes first.
- **Use your own words** to show you understand. Never copy out whole phrases and sentences, but you can't change words like 'cobbled'.
- When the question says 'Write about 120–160 words in total', it is a guide to help you know how much to write. A few more or less won't matter.

STEP 3 — Notes and a sample answer.
Before you read them, answer the question yourself.

Make notes like this:

Normal
- boy with barrow/goatsmeat/ "clanging"
- steep main street/ narrow, "twisting"
- cobbled
- quiet
- square
- town hall
- streets go up hill
- monastery on top
- mountains (dark? stony) at back
- few people (on foot) in town
- famous for handmade ("miniature") furniture

Carnival
- farmers come to town
- smart taxis
- tourists
- donkeys and bicycles
- engine noise/ 3-wheelers
- general noise and crowds
- cafes erected
- colourful dress
- waving blue/ white flags
- square filled with dancers
- earshattering
- fantastic goat costumes
- cacophony of goat bells

SAMPLE ANSWER

If you visit Skyros, you see the Town Hall in the square and narrow cobbled streets leading steeply uphill to the monastery. Behind are the mountains. The town is quiet with only a few people walking around. Some shops sell handmade miniature furniture, and you may see a boy delivering goatsmeat in a wheelbarrow.

On carnival day the square fills with farmers, smart Athenians and children waving national flags. There are temporary eating places and noise and movement everywhere. Three-wheeled farm vehicles, big taxis, bicycles and donkeys compete for space. When the wild dancers in their outlandish goat costumes explode on the town, there is an ear-shattering cacophony of bronze goatbells.

Early days

There is no doubt that teaching is a demanding job. Recent research shows that a fair number of those trained for it are not taking teaching jobs at the end of their courses. Others are leaving after a short period, and for some this is the right decision. However, many of those who leave have lost the chance of a rewarding career. With thought and good advice early difficulties can be overcome, and the decision to join the teaching profession confirmed as correct.

One of the major reasons for the rejection of teaching at an early stage is that of disappointed expectations. This often happens because pupils are indifferent or hostile when it was thought that they would be friendly and responsive. Many new teachers have made job satisfaction depend upon making an impact in the first few months of teaching; and when this does not happen they lose enthusiasm.

Most teachers are in the job because they care about young people and want to enhance their lives. However, the skills needed to do this are not easy to acquire. While they are developing it is wise to aim for a competent standard of teaching rather than attempt brilliance. If ambitious attempts to win over pupils have gone wrong then it is a good thing to set more moderate targets.

Essential to the teacher is an ability to form relationships with individuals who vary greatly in background, appearance and behaviour. The new teacher is often discouraged because there is no sign of this happening, and yet knows from life outside school that worthwhile relationships cannot usually be formed quickly. Until pupils are known and understood reasonably well (they can never be understood completely!) the most effective teaching cannot take place. Frenzied activity and worrying over whether an ambitious lesson is successful can make any sort of effective communication with the class very difficult.

It is better to use quiet, structured activities which give you an opportunity to get to know the class by talking to them as individuals.

Another way in which a young teacher can ease the pressure is by having a sensible attitude to time. Teaching without preparation is bad, but so is teaching when exhausted by too much: a balance must be found. A reasonable period of rest every day and at the weekend is essential. Avoid being dominated by the need always to mark and return work for the next lesson.

Another problem arises when the seriousness of it all overtakes you and prevents any glimmer of humour getting through. Of course the whole business is very important, but there are times when seeing the funny side of things is just what is needed, both with the pupils and when talking about the job to others.

Any teaching situation is made up of a variety of factors, and all these need to be considered when working out how to improve as a teacher. Don't respond to failure by concluding that you are hopeless, when in fact very often there is a simple reason for what has happened. For example, the content of the lesson might show that the pupils were being expected to cope with material which was too simple or, more likely, too advanced. Or perhaps what at the time seemed a small break in the lesson to find a piece of equipment badly affected concentration. It is a good idea to look for straightforward explanations before searching the soul about one's suitability for teaching.

by Peter Freeman

How to make a summary – in six steps

 **STEP 4** *More helpful details for you to remember*

Write your answer

Question: *Summarise the reasons why young teachers sometimes find it difficult and discouraging when they start work.*

Write about 120–160 words in total.

Which words in the questions should you highlight?

The article is a little wordy. You'll need skill to find the **reasons** and express them **concisely** in your own words.

Select only what you need to answer the question. **Reasons** – not advice to young teachers.

Did you highlight **reasons, difficult,** and **discouraging**? Write your notes below. The first two have already been done.

Notes

1 They find teaching very different from what they expected.

2 They find pupils unwilling to learn (indifferent) and unfriendly.

3

4

5

6

7

8

9

10

Dutch see advantages in car-free centres

Traffic congestion has led to radical planning

Where most cities snarl and roar, Groningen ticks, squeaks, rattles and (occasionally) rings its bell. This is because in Groningen – the Netherlands' sixth largest city – the bicycle is the main form of transport.

Sixteen years ago ruinous traffic congestion led Groningen to dig up its city-centre motorways in pursuit of an ideal – the 'compact city'. Last year it embarked on the creation of a car-free city centre. Its motives, however, repay examination.

'This is not an environmental programme,' Gerrit van Werven, a senior city planner, said. 'It is an economic programme. We are boosting jobs and business. It has been proved that planning for the bicycle is cheaper than planning for the car.'

Groningen, a city of 170,000, has the highest level of bicycle usage in the West. Fifty-seven per cent of its inhabitants travel by bicycle – compared with four per cent in the UK.

Since September 1977, when a six-lane motorway intersection in the city's historic city centre was replaced by greenery, pedestrianisation, cycleways and bus lanes, the city has staged a remarkable recovery. Rents are among the highest in the Netherlands, the outflow of population has been reversed and businesses, once in revolt against car restraint, are clamouring for more of it.

A vital threshold has also been crossed. Through sheer weight of numbers, the bicycle lays down the rules, slowing down the traffic, colouring the attitudes of drivers. According to Mr van Werven, this demonstrates the 'important law ... [that] the more cycling there is, the safer it becomes.'

A half-hour ride round the city shows roads being narrowed or closed to traffic, cycleways under construction, and new housing to which the only direct access is by cycle. All new buildings must provide cycle garages: there are thousands of spaces in bike-parks. Out-of-town shopping centres are banned. The aim is to force cars to take longer detours but to provide a 'fine-mesh' network for bicycles, giving them easy access to the city centre.

'We don't ride bicycles because we are poor – people here are richer than in England. We ride them because it is fun, it is faster, it is convenient,' Mr van Werven said.

Like the Netherlands nationally, Groningen is backing bicycles because of fears about car growth. Its 10-year bicycle investment programme is costing G20 million, yet every commuter car it keeps off the road saves at least G500 a year in 'hidden' costs, such as noise, pollution, parking and health.

Rattlesnake expert

William Brown *shares his experiences and discusses the relationship between humans and rattlesnakes*

By late September in the mountains of the North East the temperature at night begins to drop. For some time before, those of us who watch for timber rattlesnakes have seen them slowly moving back toward their dens. We know that some will be caught out and die. Others will be blindly killed by people.

The first protracted cold spell 'pushes them in', as we say; by mid-October the snakes are in their dens. It will be another six or seven months – spent in constant darkness in soil spaces, holes and crevices below the freezing line – before the warm days of late April and early May entice the snakes out of hibernation. Meanwhile, those who have a fear of rattlers will be walking easier through the woods.

How to make a summary – in six steps

Finding rattlesnake dens, always a memorable activity, sometimes provides rare excitement. Early one May I climbed up among fallen rocks in a steep ravine, then sat down to write notes. Suddenly the stillness was broken up by a loud whirring rattle about 40 feet upslope.

Climbing across brush-choked boulders towards the sound, I glimpsed the rattler's disappearing tail, oscillating furiously in a crevice beyond reach. Listening closely, I could hear a second snake rattling underground. Then, about 30 feet away in another direction, a third rattler sounded off. I felt surrounded! As I stood jotting down my observations, I glanced down. Right at my feet a large rattlesnake lay coiled motionless and nearly invisible in the leaves!

I had stumbled across a den area and within an hour I had seen ten rattlers and caught seven for research in the laboratory.

As a venomous animal capable of causing death in a human, the rattlesnake has always aroused fear.

The fact is that the timber rattlesnake will almost always retreat from an encounter with man and, if surprised, normally issues a warning with the characteristic whir-r-r-r of its vibrating tail. The snake rarely strikes humans except in self-defence. Almost anyone willing to set aside his snake aversion can accept rattlesnakes as marvellously suited predators, functioning in the natural environment as rodent controllers.

Rattlesnakes, however, are often among the most vulnerable to unnatural agencies of mortality, notably humans.

The main factors are unregulated 'sport' hunting, commercial collecting for the live animal trade, market and bounty hunting, and campaigns of extermination.

To see one of these snakes coiled on the forest floor or lying peacefully on a remote mountain ledge is to gain a glimpse of a treasured but diminishing wilderness world. As a splendid exemplar of our natural heritage, the timber rattlesnake should be left undisturbed in its remaining habitats.

Answer the questions and practise for a better grade

Question: *Summarise the changes that have been made in Groningen to make the bicycle the most important form of transport, and the advantages that this has brought to the city and its people.*

Write about 150–200 words in total.

Question: *Summarise the evidence that William Brown is an expert, an enthusiast and an environmentalist.*

Write about 150–200 words in total.

Ideas for revision

What the examiners look for

What have you learned about writing a summary? Fill in the cues below.

Highlight the important ....

Select only information that is ....

Use your own .... if possible

Don't use unnecessary .... Be concise

Make any necessary changes to the order of ....

How to comment on content and style – in six steps

Read the passage and then follow Steps 1 to 3 to a better grade.

Eleven-year old Amy has a kick like a donkey ... she can't find a girls' football team to play a match with

Give us a game!
by Sean Moriarty

Amy Shipton lives for football. Every inch of her bedroom wall is covered with posters of her sporting heroes and she spends most of her spare time kicking a ball around.

But the 11-year-old is not happy. Since moving to Simon Langton Girls' School where football is not on the curriculum, the sport she loves has been given the red card.

Amy, who lives in Castle Street, Canterbury, has become so desperate to play a match, she wants to move to another school where she can play football.

Now mum Lesley has asked *Adscene* to help find a team in which Amy can compete.

'Amy takes after her father; she has always been football mad. Since she was old enough to walk, she has been kicking footballs,' she said.

'While other little girls were playing with dollies, she was playing football with the boys.

I believe that Simon Langton is the best place for Amy to get an education. We don't want to change schools, but it is such a shame she is being denied the sport she loves.

She played football in friendly matches when she was at the Hersden and St Stephen's Primary schools and her games teachers called her their secret weapon. Amy's got a kick like a donkey and is really very good at the game.'

Lesley says she would like to hear from anyone who runs a girls' football team, or is thinking of setting one up.

'I thought about setting up a team myself, but I haven't got the time it would take to do it properly,' she said.

'I don't mind travelling to take Amy to play. It would be worth it for how happy it would make her.'

'Not allowing girls of my age to play competitive football is sexist,' said Amy.

'Girls are just as good at football as boys. Something should be done to change these out-of-date laws.'

The Football Association said it actively encouraged girls to take up the sport.

'We don't allow mixed competitive football at secondary school age because we want to encourage the growth of girls-only football teams, and you don't do this by allowing the girls to play in boys' teams,' said FA spokesman David Bloomfield.

'It's nonsense to say we are sexist in our approach – we are here to increase the number of people who play and watch football, and to maintain its popularity at all levels among both sexes.'

Anthony Stanton, head teacher at Simon Langton Girls, said there was a limit to how many sports his school could offer.

'We do offer as much sport as we can to complement our busy academic curriculum,' he said.

'The problem of introducing new sports is that it can spread our resources too thin, and we might find that splitting up the girls makes it difficult to field a team in any sport.

We realise many of our pupils pursue other sporting interests outside school hours, and I wish Amy every luck with finding a football club to play for.'

(Adapted from articles in Adscene, September 1994, by kind permission of Adscene Publishing Ltd.)

Promising footballer Amy Shipton is desperate to find a football club to play for.

How to comment on content and style – in six steps

 **Look closely at this question**

Question: *The writer wants us to sympathise with Amy Shipton.*

How does he set out to do this?

You should comment on:

▸ the **layout**

▸ the **views** of Antony Stanton and David Bloomfield, as well as those of Amy and her mother

▸ the writer's **choice of words**.

Write about 180–230 words in total.

Support your comments by referring to the text.

(Don't be put off by the length. Think about the words that are highlighted.)

 **How to answer the question**

▸ Comment on the passage; **don't** summarise facts and ideas.

▸ Give answers to all three headings (layout, views, choice of words).

▸ Find as many answers as possible. Don't take one or two ideas and write about them at great length.

▸ For each answer, quote some words to **support** (explain, prove) what you say.

▸ Look for words and phrases that stand out for you and explain why.

 **Some notes**

1 Layout

▸ Sympathetic headline grabs attention.

▸ Picture of Amy (glum)/professional-looking football.

2 Characters' views

▸ Amy's enthusiasm ('Every inch of her bedroom wall...') and crusading spirit ('out of date laws') but desperate ('wants to move to another school').

▸ No. 1 supporter, 'Mum Lesley' helps her: 'be worth it for how happy it would make her'.

▸ FA like cross teacher/'Don't allow', 'It's nonsense'.

▸ Headteacher, kindly but grudging/'limit to how many sports'.

3 Language

victimisation 'Given the red card', 'denied the sport she loves'

power (to show how good she is) 'kick like a donkey', 'secret weapon'

emotion 'lives for football', 'sport she loves', 'desperate to play'

Use these notes to help you write your answer.

Aaargh!

I have a plan. It might work. Next time you are lying in a dentist's chair looking up into those cold, fish-like eyes staring down into your mouth, why not try picturing the world from the dentist's side of the drill?

Imagine what it must be like to have customers hating every second spent in your company. To walk into the surgery and see sad, nervous people, half paralysed with fear as they flick dolefully through the pages of once-glossy magazines, their brains scrambled by loathing for the dentist and a longing to walk free.

The problem for patients and dentists stems from the fact that a simple filling involves an assault on all five senses.

Sight: the awful expanse of ceiling, the ET-like light, the harrowing posters warning of the dangers of sweets, demanding correct tooth-brushing and offering pictures of gum disease.

Smell: that smell. Who can do anything other than gag? How can a clean smell be so grizzly – that blend of lino polish, mouthwash and surgical soap?

Hearing: the noise of the drill assaults the ear even as you open the door. Other sounds are equally loathsome: that unique squeak of a nurse's shoe on polished lino; the flip, flip, flip of the man not reading the motoring magazine; the mewling of a frightened child or grown man; the hubble bubble of a fish tank. I hate fish tanks. Dentists think that pulse rates and adrenaline levels drop in the presence of a fish tank. Not mine. The fish glare back at me with dentists' eyes that say: 'Soon you will suffer.'

Taste: nothing quite matches the taste of a rubber glove as it probes and pushes its way around, hauling gums back to make room for a cart-load of ironmongery. Mouthwash, always pink, would still taste foul even if they flavoured it with whisky and peanut butter.

Touch: the most intense experience of all, for hot on its heels comes pain. Ever noticed how dentists never use the word pain? At dental school they are drilled (sorry) with a lexicon of alternatives. You feel only 'slight discomfort' in a dentist's surgery. As the probe goes in, jabbing away at a tooth that has never given a day's trouble in its life, a dentist will ask, 'Is it tender when I do this?' What is the function of that probe – to find points of weakness or to create them?

'Ah ha!' says the dentist, smiling enigmatically as you lurch back in the chair following one spectacularly successful exploration: 'A little sensitive I see.' 'Only when some sadist gives it a ruddy great jab,' would be your reply, were it not for the pile of junk he has loaded into your mouth. Odd, isn't it, how dental equipment swells in size once it reaches your mouth? Delicate cotton wool wads grow to the size of carpet rolls and suction probes become oil pipelines. All you can manage is an incoherent, 'Uh huh'.

You think the dentist is not aware of all this? Of course he is. It may be hard to believe, but dentists are human too. It is not possible to spend all day working with highly-stressed people without absorbing some of the stress yourself. Dentists, along with doctors and vets, figure well up in the suicide stakes.

It is an extremely lonely job. Many practices have just one dentist. There is no one around to moan to. There is no positive feedback. When was the last time you said to your dentist 'Thanks old chap. You do really nice work'? I certainly haven't. As soon as it's over I get out of the place. There are few feelings to match the sense of relief at leaving a surgery.

Dentistry can also be very boring. One dentist I endured would mumble a constant stream of inanities to himself. 'A pitcher at one with himself,' he would intone, or 'The medic does not always buy books.' After two years of this I had to ask. '*Times* crossword' was his reply.

by Dylan Winter

How to comment on content and style – in six steps

More helpful details for you to remember

Question: *The writer of Aaargh! aims to show that a dentist's life and the experiences of patients are equally unpleasant.*

How does he do this?

Support your comments by referring to the passage.

Ask yourself:

▶ What effect does the writer try to make on you?

▶ Which words in the passage make this effect?

Look below at some of the ways writers can use words.

Ye loathsome sinners, the end of the world approaches with bloodshed, death and damnation!

Frighten you
Intimidate you

Imagine these poor defenceless animals imprisoned in cruel cages, cramped, nowhere to move ...

With Torrid Timeshares you can relax on your own far away, tropical island, with only the whispers of the palm trees and the distant sound of the coral reef ...

To make you sad, sympathetic or angry

Mouthwash would still taste foul even if they flavoured it with whisky and peanut butter.

To entertain you. To amuse

To persuade, attract, exaggerate with bias, halftruths, propaganda

SAMPLE ANSWERS

1 The writer of the article shows that the life of a dentist and the experiences of his patients are unpleasant by describing what it is like at the dentist's and what he does to you. For example he says that the posters are about disease and there are nasty noises in the waiting room and the surgery. He doesn't like it the dentist peering at him and poking piles of junk in his mouth.

2 The writer uses exaggerated language throughout: posters are "harrowing" and clean smells "grizzly". Some of the exaggeration is also humorous, for example the "cartload of ironmongery" that goes in your mouth. All this is supposed to reinforce the idea of fear and discomfort but at the same time is signalling that it should not be taken too seriously.

The writer also makes the reader think that all dentists have "cold, fishlike eyes" and are "enigmatic" and "sadists". Reading this we are tempted to forget that dentists are real, kindly people.

Which is better, and why?

Aegean Turkey

Cruise the inshore coastline of Aegean Turkey on board the Swiss managed 'Tall Ship' the SV Druzhba

There can surely be no better way to explore the idyllic and unspoilt coastline of Turkey than from the comfort of the motorised and sailing vessel, SV Druzhba which combines all the comforts of a normal cruise vessel with the added experience of travelling under sail when the weather conditions permit.

Sailing from Antalya, we will journey along the wild and beautiful coastline of Lycia and in addition to visiting the better known ancient sites, we go to some romantic places which travellers hardly ever see.

Being ship-borne enables us to visit the most attractive and remote harbours and move slowly through the scenes of half-sunken buildings east of Kas. Nature, ruins and relaxation form the central part of this tour. However, three days in Istanbul, that most endlessly captivating of cities will be busy and absorbing, taking in the incomparable sights from the exquisite Haghia Sophia to the splendours of Topkapi Palace.

THE SV DRUZHBA

The vessel has recently been acquired under a long term arrangement by Leisure Cruises of Switzerland and is managed by ICH, the Swiss cruise and hotel management company who are responsible for providing services of the highest standard for our river journeys in a number of places throughout the world.

All 27 cabins are outside facing with similar dimensions to those of a river vessel. All the cabins are twin berthed, with air-conditioning and ensuite facilities. Amongst the many public facilities there is a sundeck with bar, swimming platform, outdoor bar, restaurant and reception.

The SV Druzhba has a gross tonnage of 2987. Constructed in 1987 in Poland, it is being completely refurbished and upgraded to international passenger standards in 1996.

She has a crew of 17 hotel and cruise management, 20 deck hands and 30 naval cadets who will man the rigging. The vessel is 108 metres long, 14 metres on the beam with a draft of 6.6 metres and a sail area of 2936 square metres. It is equipped with tender vessels for excursion visits and possesses the latest navigational and safety aids including SATCOM satellite fax and telephone.

A truly unique travel experience.

St John Ambulance is one of our best-known charities. Read this extract from an appeal for money.

A small price to pay

As well as providing essential First Aid support at public events, St John Ambulance fund training and youth programmes throughout the country. We also invest time, care and energy in the community, improving the quality of life for countless individuals. And then, of course, there are the ambulances and vital equipment we require to continue our lifesaving work.

These are all reasons why we must ask for your help today.

You simply can't put a value on a life, and if we save just one life a day, make life easier, more comfortable or more worthwhile for one individual, then the investment is more than justified. We feel sure you'll agree.

Brought back to life

Mike Davies is particularly grateful to members of St John Ambulance who literally brought him 'back to life'.

Mike collapsed just yards from the finishing line of the Fleet Half Marathon with a heart attack, but St John Ambulance volunteers raced over and began immediate resuscitation. Mike knows that without St John Ambulance, he simply wouldn't be here today to tell the tale. He says: 'They are always there, but it's not until this sort of thing happens that you appreciate just how important they are.'

Make sure we're always here to care

Mike Davies was one of the lucky ones. St John Ambulance volunteers were able to reach and treat him quickly, drawing on their professional training and the equipment available in their ambulance.

But what if, because of lack of funds, there's no-one trained to reach a casualty, or we haven't got the modern resources we need to treat someone quickly and effectively?

We will always, of course, continue to do our best and we try never to let anyone down. But the difficulty facing us today is so great that I can only hope that you in turn won't let **us** down in our hour of need – **and help make sure we're always here when you need us**.

Please support our urgent appeal for funds

St John Ambulance really is Britain's 'lifesaving charity', and, whilst I appreciate that there are probably a great many demands on your generosity already, I do hope I can ask you to support our urgent appeal today.

The crisis is upon us **now**, so we must ask you to help us quickly. Whatever you are able to send will help us make sure we're always here to care. **And give our hard-working, selfless volunteers the vital backup they need to carry on their lifesaving work**.

by Sir David Parry-Evans GCB CBE

THE OCR NON-FICTION AND MEDIA TEXTS PAPER

STEP 5 — Answer the questions and practise for a better grade

Question: *In what ways is the holiday in Aegean Turkey made to sound attractive?*

You should comment on:

▶ the way details of the cruise and of the vessel have been chosen

▶ the language used in the advertisement.

Question: *In what ways does the appeal try to persuade you that it would be a good idea to give money to St John Ambulance?*

You should consider:

▶ what the appeal tells you

▶ the way it says it

▶ the way the words are presented on the page.

STEP 6 — Ideas for revision

Persuasiveness

You've looked at four passages. Choose the two which you thought tried to persuade you the most.

1

2

For each one, write down what you thought was the strongest thing they did to persuade you.

1

2

Fairness

Answer these questions with your opinion: Yes (✓) No (✗) Not sure (?)

	Give us a game	**Aaargh!**	**Aegean Turkey**	**A small price to pay**
Was the passage truthful?				
Did it tell you all the information you needed?				
Was it fair to both sides of the argument?				

Using words

Name two of the passages where you thought words were used well.

1   2

For each one say why and give an example of what you mean.

1

2

20

How to write an argument

Look again at the pre-released material on page 7.

Good and bad neighbours

The question may require you to write in one of these forms:

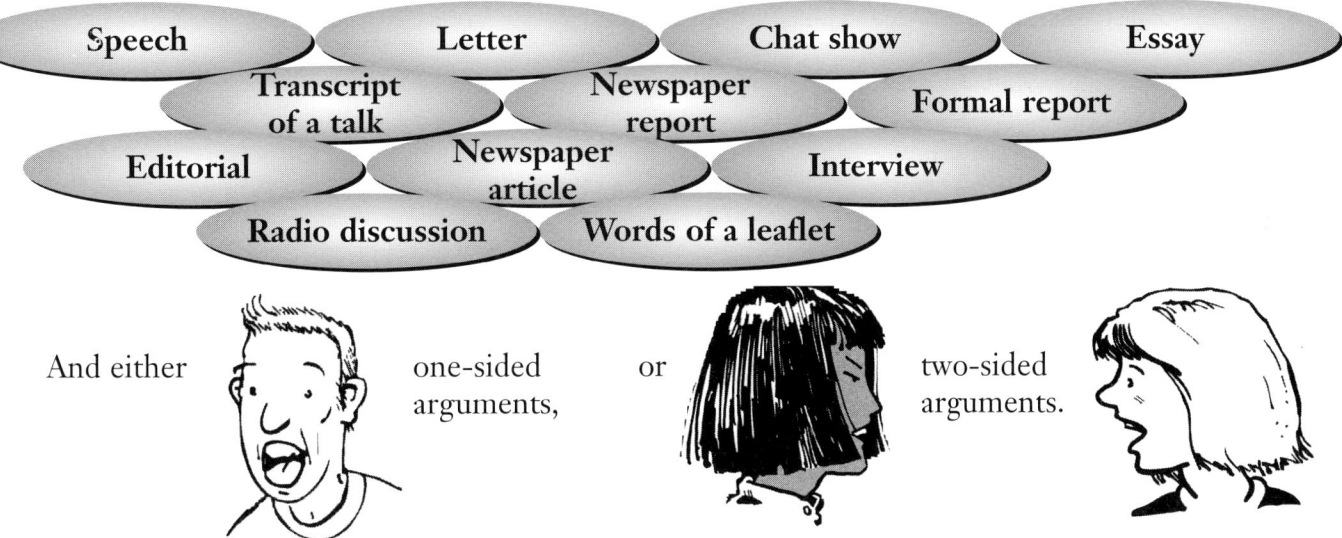

- Speech
- Letter
- Chat show
- Essay
- Transcript of a talk
- Newspaper report
- Formal report
- Editorial
- Newspaper article
- Interview
- Radio discussion
- Words of a leaflet

And either one-sided arguments, or two-sided arguments.

Examples of questions

▶ Why is good neighbourliness important?

▶ A politician, a police inspector and a housewife meet on TV to discuss the importance of being good neighbours. The presenter puts two questions to them:

Is it possible for people to be good neighbours?

Why is it important that they should try?

Write the script of what they say. Let the presenter speak first.

▶ Every year we read of old people dying of cold in their lonely homes or children who are mistreated – and no one seems to know or care. Write an article for a local newspaper, arguing for more interest and vigilance by neighbours.

▶ Two neighbours meet over the garden fence. One accuses the other of anti-social behaviour while the other thinks his rights are being challenged. Write their arguments and show how they resolve the issue.

▶ Write a letter to your local council complaining about the increasingly thoughtless behaviour of people who live in your (or an imaginary) street, and arguing ways of improving the situation.

Good and bad arguments

Bad arguments go round in circles and repeat themselves – or can be broken up and put together again any old how.

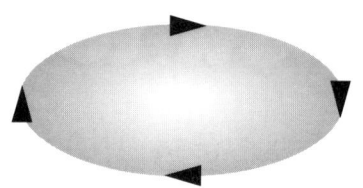

Good arguments know where they are going and get there by degrees:

STEP 3 Link your paragraphs

STEP 2 Get your ideas in order and develop them

STEP 1 Plan

The plan

Title: Why is good neighbourliness important?
Brainstorm it and add some of your own ideas.

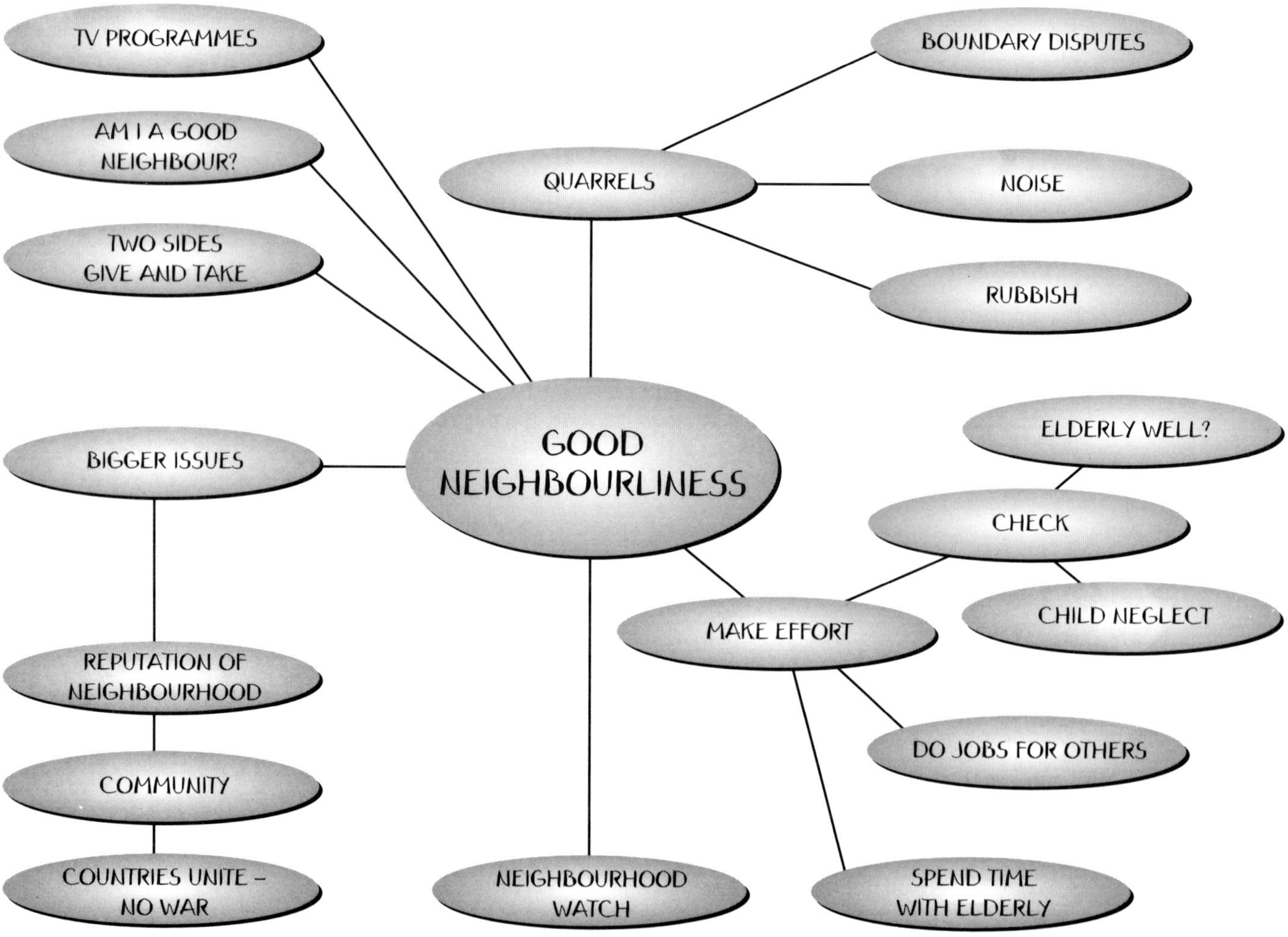

Get your ideas in order and develop them

- 1 Description of a good neighbour
- 2 Description of a bad neighbour
- 3 Me! Give and take Selfishness
- 4 What if everyone were selfish?
- 5 Ways of building communities

Link your paragraphs

To me a good neighbour is someone who does not mind that I live next door and who tolerates my eccentricities...

On the other hand I might be less lucky and finish up with one of those people they call the 'Neighbour from Hell'...

But the person I ought to be writing about is ME...

So are my neighbours only the people who live next door..?

Therefore it would be better if we all made an effort to live together as friends...

This is just one way of planning and writing a response.

What the examiners look for

- ▶ varied material and original thought
- ▶ properly developed paragraphs with clear links between
- ▶ a wide range of vocabulary (don't repeat 'neighbours' too often)
- ▶ well built sentences – varied – some shorter, some longer
- ▶ spelling and use of full stops correct, work checked for carelessness

2 THE OCR LITERARY TEXTS PAPER

What the exam requires: other cultures

Read	Write
A story from another culture*	Q1 Comments on key features (character, meaning, setting, plot and style).
	Q2 Use the story as a starting point (marked only for writing).
	Q3 A story or some personal writing.

*The story will be available to study about twelve weeks before the exam.

What is meant by other cultures?

The story will be like any other – about people, their experiences and their emotions. It will come from another part of the world – like the United States, the Caribbean, Africa, Asia, Russia where people have different traditions and ways of life. If this is important to the story, you must point it out in your answer.

Ten important things about other cultures

Think about these points as you read the story.

1 Differences in attitudes to birth, marriage and death.

2 Differences in family life – like discipline, how children are treated and whether the old are respected.

3 The sort of education and its importance to parents and children.

4 The importance of religion and what is right and wrong.

5 How weather affects people's lives.

6 Rich and poor – people's lifestyles and expectations.

7 Village customs, like the ways communities deal with crime.

8 The place of men and women – how free are women to live independently and to make their own decisions?

9 Whether people of different races live well together.

10 The way people address each other and the type of language they use.

Stories from other cultures – in six steps

Read this passage and then follow Steps 1 to 3 to a better grade.

This is the beginning of a story called 'The First Party' by *Attia Hosain*. While you read it, think of the reasons the wife behaves as she does and what the other guests think of her.

A matter of acute embarrassment

After the dimness of the veranda, the bewildering brightness of the room made her stumble against the unseen doorstep. Her nervousness edged towards panic, and the darkness seemed a forsaken friend, but her husband was already steadying her into the room.

'My wife,' he said in English, and the alien sounds softened the awareness of this new relationship.

The smiling, tall woman came towards them with outstretched hands and she put her own limply into the other's firm grasp.

'How d'you do?' said the woman.

'How d'you do?' said the fat man beside her.

'I am very well, thank you,' she said in the low voice of an uncertain child repeating a lesson. Her shy glance avoided their eyes.

They turned to her husband, and in the warm current of their friendly ease she stood coldly self-conscious.

'I hope we are not too early,' her husband said.

'Of course not; the others are late. Do sit down.'

She sat on the edge of the big chair, her shoulders drooping, nervously pulling her sari over her head as the weight of its heavy gold embroidery pulled it back.

'What will you drink?' the fat man asked her.

'Nothing, thank you.'

'Cigarette?'

'No, thank you.'

Her husband and the tall woman were talking about her, she felt sure. Pin-points of discomfort pricked her and she smiled to hide them.

The woman held a wineglass in one hand and a cigarette in the other. She wondered how it felt to hold a cigarette with such self-confidence; to flick the ash with such assurance. The woman had long nails, pointed and scarlet. She looked at her own – unpainted, cut carefully short – wondering how anyone could eat, work, wash with those claws dipped in blood. She drew her sari over her hands, covering her rings and bracelets, noticing the other's bare wrists, like a widow's.

'Shy little thing, isn't she, but charming,' said the woman as if soothing a frightened child.

'She'll get over it soon. Give me time,' her husband laughed. She heard him and blushed, wishing to be left unobserved and grateful for the diversion when other guests came in.

She did not know whether she was meant to stand up when they were being introduced, and shifted uneasily in the chair, half rising; but her husband came and stood by her, and by the pressure of his hand on her shoulder she knew she must remain sitting.

She was glad when polite formality ended and they forgot her for their drinks, their cigarettes, their talk and laughter. She shrank into her chair, lonely in her strangeness yet dreading approach. She felt curious eyes on her and her discomfort multiplied them. When anyone came and sat by her she smiled in cold defence, uncertainty seeking refuge in silence, and her brief answers crippled conversation. She found the bilingual patchwork distracting, and its pattern, familiar to others, with allusions and references unrelated to her own experiences, was distressingly obscure. Overheard light chatter appealing to her woman's mind brought no relief of understanding. Their different stresses made even talk of dress and appearance sound unfamiliar. She could not understand the importance of relating clothes to time and place and not just occasion; nor their preoccupation with limbs and bodies, which should be covered, and not face and features alone. They made problems about things she took for granted.

Her bright rich clothes and heavy jewellery oppressed her when she saw the simplicity of their clothes. She wished she had not dressed so, even if it was the custom, because no one seemed to care for customs, or even know them, and looked at her as if she were an object on display. Her discomfort changed to uneasy defiance, and she stared at the strange creatures around her. But her swift eyes slipped away in timid shyness if they met another's.

Her husband came at intervals that grew longer with a few gay words, or a friend to whom he proudly presented 'My wife'. She noticed the never-empty glass in his hand, and the smell of his breath, and from shock and distress she turned to disgust and anger. It was wicked, it was sinful to drink, and she could not forgive him.

She could not make herself smile any more but no one noticed and their unconcern soured her anger. She did not want to be disturbed and was tired of the persistent 'Will you have a drink?', 'What will you drink?', 'Sure you won't drink?' It seemed they objected to her not drinking, and she was confused by this reversal of values. She asked for a glass of orange juice and used it as protection, putting it to her lips when anyone came near.

They were eating now, helping themselves from a table by the wall. She did not want to leave her chair, and wondered if it was wrong and they would notice she was not eating. In her confusion she saw a girl coming towards her, carrying a small tray. She sat up stiffly and took the proffered plate with a smile.

'Do help yourself,' the girl said and bent forward. Her light sari slipped from her shoulder and the tight red silk blouse outlined each high breast. She pulled her own sari closer round her, blushing. The girl, unaware, said, 'Try this sandwich, and the olives are good.'

She had never seen an olive before but did not want to admit it, and when she put it in her mouth she wanted to spit it out. When no one was looking, she slipped it under her chair, then felt sure someone had seen her and would find it.

Look closely at this question

Question: *What impressions does the writer give of the wife and her feelings about the party?*

You should consider:

▶ the appearance and behaviour of the other guests

▶ how her husband's behaviour differs from hers

▶ her reactions to what she sees and hears.

IMPRESSIONS
Effects on your mind or emotions

BEHAVIOUR
What they do or say

APPEARANCE
What they look like, how they're dressed

REACTIONS
Feelings or thoughts in response

STEP 2 — How to answer the question

▶ Respond to the main part of the question – the first two lines.

▶ Look for **detail** to use in your answer. The examiners will give the highest marks to detailed, relevant answers.

STEP 3 — Some rough notes

Use these notes to write a practice answer.

Impression of the wife

▶ She's ill at ease.
▶ Later she becomes defiant.
▶ She realises she doesn't belong because of her culture.
▶ Does the writer make you sympathise with her?

Appearance and behaviour of guests

▶ The hostess's welcome.
▶ The women have painted fingernails, bare wrists, wear revealing clothes.
▶ They talk behind her back and try to make her drink.

Husband's behaviour

▶ Steadies her into the room and keeps her sitting when introduced.
▶ Seems proud of her.
▶ Smells of drink.

You need to work out the **reasons** for the wife's reactions and find **quotations** in the passage to support the notes.

Write your additional notes and quotations here.

THE OCR LITERARY TEXTS PAPER

Read this passage and then follow Step 4 to a better grade.

This is a description of the lavish parties given by Jay Gatsby. It comes from the novel 'The Great Gatsby' by *F. Scott-Fitzgerald*. This time, useful notes for answering the question have been written in the margin.

The Great Gatsby

There was music from my neighbour's house through the summer nights. In his blue gardens men and girls came and went like <u>moths</u> among the whisperings and the <u>champagne</u> and <u>the stars</u>. At high tide in the afternoon, I watched his guests diving from the tower of his raft, or taking the sun on the hot sand of his beach while his <u>two motor-boats</u> slit the waters of the Sound, drawing aquaplanes over cataracts of foam. On week-ends his <u>Rolls-Royce</u> became an omnibus, bearing parties to and from the city between nine in the morning and long past midnight, while his station wagon scampered like a brisk yellow bug to meet all trains. And on Mondays <u>eight servants</u>, including an extra gardener, toiled all day with mops and scrubbing-brushes and hammers and garden-shears, repairing the ravages of the night before.

— the narrator is Gatsby's neighbour
— rich, romantic!
— extremely rich!

numbering the staff
— almost humorously shows off size

   Every Friday five crates of oranges and lemons arrived from a fruiterer in New York – every Monday these same oranges and lemons left his back door in a pyramid of pulpless halves. There was a machine in the kitchen which could extract the juice of two hundred oranges in half an hour if a little button was pressed two hundred times by a butler's thumb.
   At least once a fortnight a <u>corps</u> of caterers came down with <u>several hundred feet of canvas</u> and <u>enough coloured lights to make a Christmas tree of</u> Gatsby's enormous garden. On buffet tables, garnished with glistening hors-d'oeuvre, spiced baked hams crowded against salads of harlequin designs and pastry turkeys <u>bewitched to a dark gold</u>. In the main hall a bar with a real brass rail was set up, and stocked with gins and liquors and with cordials so long forgotten that most of his female guests were too young to know one from another.

so does the eccentric detail of the oranges, the caterers and the canvas

fine description of exotic food.
bewitched = magic!
— range of drinks

   By seven o'clock the orchestra has arrived, no thin five-piece affair, but a whole pitful of oboes and trombones and saxophones and viols and cornets and piccolos, and low and high drums. The last swimmers have come in from the beach now and are dressing upstairs; the cars from New York are parked five deep in the drive, and already the halls and salons and verandas are <u>gaudy with primary colours</u>, and hair bobbed in strange new ways, and shawls beyond the dreams of Castile. The bar is in full swing, and floating rounds of cocktails permeate the garden outside, until the air is alive with chatter and laughter, and casual innuendo and introductions forgotten on the spot, and enthusiastic meetings between women who never knew each other's names.
   The lights grow brighter as the earth <u>lurches</u> away from the sun, and now the orchestra is playing yellow cocktail music, and the <u>opera</u> of voices pitches a key higher. <u>Laughter is easier minute by minute, spilled</u>

— typical U.S. big band
almost a still from a period U.S. movie
— fashion

— socialising

— as if drunk
— another nice image (they are talking, not singing)

with prodigality, tipped out at a cheerful word. The groups change more swiftly, swell with new arrivals, dissolve and form in the same breath; already there are wanderers, confident girls who weave here and there among the stouter and more stable, become for a sharp, joyous moment the centre of a group, and then, excited with triumph, glide on through the sea-change of faces and voices and colour under the constantly changing light. *[increasing excitement of conversation]*

Suddenly one of these gypsies, in trembling opal, seizes a cocktail out of the air, dumps it down for courage and, moving her hands like Frisco, dances out alone on the canvas platform. A momentary hush; the orchestra leader varies his rhythm obligingly for her, and there is a burst of chatter as the erroneous news goes around that she is Gilda Gray's understudy from the Follies. The party has begun. *[romantic? / U.S. showbiz reference]*

I believe that on the first night I went to Gatsby's house I was one of the few guests who had actually been invited. People were not invited – they went there. They got into automobiles which bore them out to Long Island, and somehow they ended up at Gatsby's door. Once there they were introduced by somebody who knew Gatsby, and after that they conducted themselves according to the rules of behaviour associated with an amusement park. Sometimes they came and went without having met Gatsby at all, came for the party with simplicity of heart that was its own ticket of admission. *[Gatsby not at his own party!]*

I have been actually invited. A chauffeur in a uniform of robins-egg blue crossed my lawn early that Saturday morning with a surprisingly formal note from his employer: the honour would be entirely Gatsby's, it said, if I would attend his 'little party' that night. He had seen me several times, and had intended to call on me long before, but a peculiar combination of circumstances had prevented it – signed Jay Gatsby, in a majestic hand. Dressed up in white flannels I went over to his lawn a little after seven, and wandered around rather ill at ease among swirls and eddies of people I didn't know – though here and there was a face I had noticed on the commuting train. I was immediately struck by the number of young Englishmen dotted about; all well dressed, all looking a little hungry, and all talking in low, earnest voices to solid and prosperous Americans. I was sure that they were selling something; bonds or insurance or automobiles. They were at least agonisingly aware of the easy money in the vicinity and convinced that it was theirs for a few words in the right key. *[understatement illustrates Gatsby's vision of life and wealth / suitable signature / fashionable, or not? / atmosphere of U.S. wealth]*

As soon as I arrived I made an attempt to find my host, but the two or three people of whom I asked his whereabouts stared at me in such an amazed way, and denied so vehemently any knowledge of his movements, that I slunk off in the directions of the cocktail table – the only place in the garden where a single man could linger without looking purposeless and alone. *[clearly one does not say this! / ironic loneliness of writer]*

THE OCR LITERARY TEXTS PAPER

 **STEP 4** *More helpful details for you to remember*

Question: *What impression does the narrator give of Jay Gatsby's 'little parties' and of the man himself?*

You should refer to:

▶ the narrator's impressions and feelings

▶ the American setting

▶ the language and style of the passage.

Find the way of note writing that suits you the best – use it for successful answers in the exam.

Try making up your own questions to help you in your answers. Here are some that have been done for you. Find details that fit the questions.

1 How do you know that the parties were not little?

2 That Jay Gatsby was incredibly rich?

3 That his parties were colourful and wild?

4 How does the description of the party remind you of American life and culture?

5 What have you learned about Gatsby himself? What does that make you think about him?

Hunters and hunted

Old man Doorne and his two elder sons walked through the swamp with the ease of men who had known the feel of mud and water all their lives. But Tonic, the youngest, splashed and stumbled every now and then. The afternoon sun, fierce and yellowing, flung shadows behind them long as fallen coconut palms. The old man was carrying his *wareshi*, an Amerindian* haversack. His back was arched and the harness bit into his forehead and shoulders.

Ahead of them was Black Bush, a belt of dense forest which rolled inland like a green ocean. Leading into Black Bush was a sandy plain where the sun had consumed and the wind swept away all but a few clumps of grass and black sage.

They approached a reed bed where bisi-bisi and wild cane had jostled the lotus lilies out of the way.

'Is how much farther we got to go?' Tonic asked plaintively.

'Don't ask stupid question, Boy, save you breath for the walk,' Doorne said.

'Nobody didn't beg you to come, so why you crying out with strain now? You, self, say you want to hunt. If you want to play man-game, then you got to take man-punishment,' Caya, the eldest said. His brother's whining angered him. It reminded him of his own tiredness.

'Ah! Lef him alone! The boy young and this swamp got teeth enough to bite the marrow of you bone out of you,' Tengar growled from deep inside his belly and he added gently, 'If you get too fatigue, boy, I will carry you over the last stretch.'

'No!' Old man Doorne shouted. 'Let the boy walk it on he own. I don't want no rice-pap mother's boy growing up under me roof.' And he turned round and glared up at his second son who towered over him like a giant mora tree over a gnarled lignum vitae.

The rise and fall of their voices and the plop-plop of their feet sounded unreal in the silence. Far to their right negrocups, swamp birds of the heron family, were grazing near a cluster of lilies. The birds stretched long necks to gaze at the intruders. A flock of ducks and curry-curries rose noisily from the bisi-bisi reeds ahead of them. But the negrocups stood moving their heads from side to side nervously and preening their wings for flight. The horizon behind those ostrich-like birds was a circle of mirages where the hazy green swamps melted away, calcinated by the sun before they merged with the sky.

As the old man and his sons drew nearer Black Bush they saw the jungle where tall trees, massed growths of bamboo and closely woven tapestries of vines and creepers had erupted out of the earth. The sight put Doorne in a good mood. In the middle of the bamboo grove was a dark hole: it was almost blocked up by new shoots but the old man recognised it. He had cut it out himself on his last trip. Huge yellow and blue butterflies danced before it. Against the dark background their wings were incandescent.

'Come on, Tonic, only lil' way to go now, boy. Brace yourself against the mud, keep you foot wide apart to fight it,' Doorne said.

'Is how much farther we got to go?' Tonic asked again and his voice was listless like a man with fever.

'Don't worry, Small-boy, I will carry you over the las' stretch,' Tengar said, stopping to hoist his brother on his broad back.

'Lef the boy alone, Tengar!' the old man said fiercely. 'He got to learn to be a hunter. Even if he bright like moonlight on still water, is time he understand he can't live by book alone. He too black and ugly to be a book man.'

'The boy is you son, old man, but he is me brother,' Tengar said.

Tonic, his legs round Tengar's waist and his hands locked around his neck, looked like a black spider clinging to a tree trunk.

*Amerindian refers to the original inhabitants of the islands

'Move out the way, old man, and stop making gar-bar*,' Tengar said, still good-natured.

'Put the boy down!' Doorne shouted, whipping out his prospecting knife.

'Old man, don't look for trouble, because when you searching for it that is the time it does ambush you. Don't bank on me vexation jus' staying in me belly and rupturing me, jus' because we is the same flesh and blood.'

Caya stepped between them and said, 'All you two making mirth or what? Look, stop this fool-acting. Old man, you better put you knife away. If the small boy too weak to bear the strain is you fault. You encourage he to full-up he head with white man book and all of we does boast how he going to turn doctor or lawyer. When turtle papa give he shell, nobody can change it.'

Growling and muttering, Doorne sheathed his knife and Tengar moved on.

'Thank you brother Tengar,' Tonic whispered and the black giant grinned showing white teeth between well-fleshed lips.

Doorne's face looked like a sky threatening rain. He thrust his head forward and strode on.

by Jan Carew

*gar-bar means trouble

Write your notes here

 **Answer the question and practise for a better grade**

Question: How does this incident illustrate the relationship between Doorne and his sons?

 **Tips for revision**

Revise your pre-released story from another culture, using these tips. **Practise** with any of the three passages you have studied.

Characters

The character that interested you the most ... Why?

A character that you sympathised with, or disliked ... Why?

Helping you to answer the question 'Why?'

- What they say.
- What they do.
- What happens to them.
- What other people say about them (true or false).

Relationships between one character and another.

Read between the lines

You sometimes have to guess details to give a full answer.

Such as ...

What people **really** mean when they speak.

What people **really** feel when good or bad things happen to them.

What happens in gaps left on purpose in the story by the writer.

What might happen as a result of the ending of a story.

Don't expect the writer to tell you every little detail: Let your imagination do some of the work!

Other cultures

Sometimes what happens to characters is affected by their own traditions and social habits.

Think about events through the eyes of the characters in the story.

Work in pairs to role play interviews with characters:

'I did it because ...'

- of my religion
- the people of my village expected it
- in our country our families always come first
- we are a superstitious people
- it is the fashion
- in my country it is dangerous to say what you believe.

THE OCR LITERARY TEXTS PAPER

How to get a better grade for the two writing questions

Read this passage and then follow Steps 1 to 3 to a better grade.

	Type	Marks	Time
Q2	Explaining, describing, arguing, giving views, etc.	20	40 mins approx.
Q3	Personal/story writing	20	40 mins approx.

The topics are linked to the reading passage.

If you allow planning and checking time, you have about 30-35 minutes writing time per task – which is not much.

How many words can you write **thoughtfully** in that time ... 250? 300? 350? Don't **ever** sacrifice quality writing for length.

Question 2

Examples of tasks

Which of the three passages on pages 25 to 32 is each of these titles linked to?

1 Do you think it is right that rich people should spend so much on their own entertainment when the poor are starving?

2 POLICE RAID SOCIETY PARTY: Write the article that would appear on the front page of the newspaper.

3 How do you feel when you see people behaving in ways that you do not like or think are right? Illustrate your answer from your own experience.

4 'I don't want no rice-pap mother's boy growing up under me roof.' Do you agree that boys should be brought up to be very tough and very strong? Argue with or against this father.

5 Should people hang on to the old ways of behaving and doing things, or should we always move with the times?

Activity

On the next two pages there are some answers to the first example: Do you think it is right that rich people should spend so much on their own entertainment when the poor are starving?

The first answer gives you an idea of what a complete answer looks like. It is about 275 words long. The other two are only parts of answers.

Decide which of the three is the best and which is the worst – and why.

How to get a better grade for the two writing questions

Question: *Do you think it is right that rich people should spend so much on their own entertainment when the poor are starving?*

Tips
- Approx 30-35 minutes actual writing time is not long to answer.
- So there is no room for wordiness – be businesslike with your ideas.

SAMPLE ANSWER

1

We live in a country where many people have more wealth than they need. Their cars are too large for their family and too fast for the speed limits. Their houses are barn-like and costly in energy. They spend vastly on their entertainment and are no better for it: do they really know the difference between wine that costs four pounds a bottle and the luxury item at eighty pounds? or really prefer the taste of caviare to cod and chips? Like the Great Gatsby they are always striving for the unattainably exciting, always reaching new heights – but to what effect?

In the end, it is our family, our friends and our feeling of ease with ourselves that we value the most. Many of us get more satisfaction digging our garden than by strolling aimlessly in the deerpark.

Somewhere at the back of our minds there lies a fit of conscience, sparked off at intervals by Comic Relief or the shocking statistics about the poor who inhabit so much of the world.

For these poor people, countless numbers of them, there is little or no future. If there were, it would probably not be worth living. They are caught in a spiral of poverty and disease, the one inviting the spread of the other. They are often the victims of ethnic war, far beyond the reach of the aid agencies that would help them. When we consider their plight, we remember with a start that we are only here by accident and that we might just as easily have been born on the foodless edge of the burning desert.

How good is this answer?

Here are some questions that the MEG examiners ask.

Answer them yourself with a ✓ (means yes)
a ? (means partly yes)
a ✗ (means no)

Are there enough ideas to be interesting?	
Do the ideas fit together to make sense?	
Are the paragraphs well built?	
Are the spelling and punctuation correct?	
Is there a good range of vocabulary?	
Do the sentences flow?	

THE OCR LITERARY TEXTS PAPER

2 — SAMPLE ANSWER

I think if you ern a lot of money you shuld do what you like with it, I mean its your's isnt it. Great Gatsby had a lot of money, he had big parties and two moter boats and anyone could go to them. They didnt have to have no invatation, they just turned up. There was lots of orange juce. Your money is your's to do what you like with it, youve erned it, noone shuld tell you what to do with it.

3 — SAMPLE ANSWER

I think rich people have worked hard for their money and should not be bullied by others to give it away. We live in a democratic country where we are free to make what we like of our lives.

There are a lot of poor people, but they live a long way away and it is up to their governments to help them. I think the charities send a lot of money to help them with food and blankets in the cold weather.

I think it would be nice to have enough money for a really good party. I could say thank you to all my family and good friends.

Even if answers 2 and 3 were complete, they would not be nearly so good as answer 1.

Which of answers 2 and 3 is the better?

Use the same way to mark them as you did for answer 1:

	Answer 2	Answer 3
Are there enough ideas to be interesting?		
Do the ideas fit together to make sense?		
Are the paragraphs well built?		
Are the spelling and punctuation correct?		
Is there a good range of vocabulary?		
Do the sentences flow?		

What the examiner says

Answer number 2 is very poor. Spelling of simple words is often wrong, commas are used for full stops and apostrophes are hopeless. The ideas are weak, barely relevant and so disordered as to make the answer difficult to read. Number 3 is better. There are no errors, but the style is weak. There are too many 'I thinks' and 'help thems'. The worst fault – and this is serious – is the lack of a properly formed paragraph. Ideas are not in a convincing order and are not satisfactorily developed.

Question 3

Examples of tasks

Which of the three passages on pages 25 to 32 is each of these titles linked to?

1 Write about an occasion when you felt lonely in a crowd.

2 Write about something you had to do which presented you with a considerable challenge.

3 Write a story in which what someone wore played a part.

4 Whatever you did, there was someone looking over your shoulder telling you what to do. Write the story.

You are free to: write exactly what happened to you
OR include something that really happened and make up the rest
OR make everything up.

Do what you need to make an event worth writing about!

Plan

How many paragraphs? Think of your reader!

Think of your language

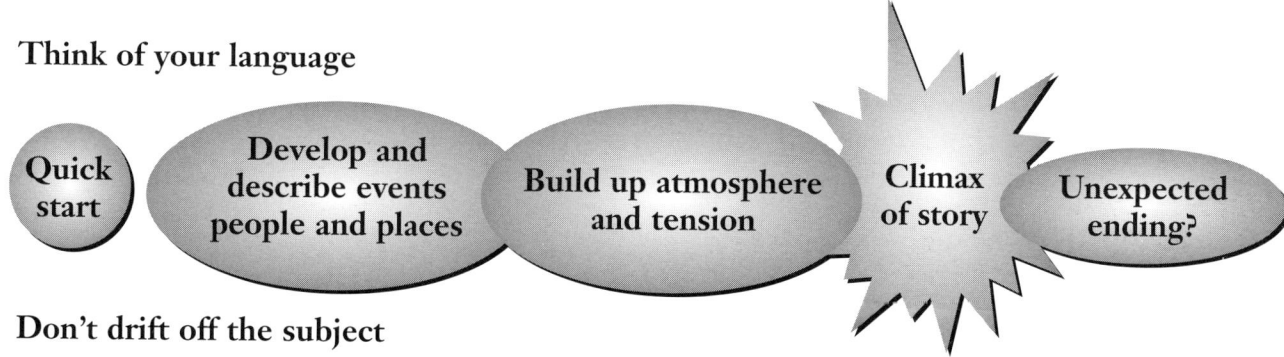

Don't drift off the subject

▶ Quick start means get to the heart of the matter! No irrelevance!

▶ In the middle interest your reader with some detail.

▶ Put the climax of the story at the end and spend enough time on it: it is the most important part. Unexpected endings are entertaining.

> **Tips**
>
> Go back and check ...
> • spelling • words missed out • full stops
> • commas • question marks • capital letters
> • carelessness
>
> If you want to cross out, use **one** line. Then write neatly over the top.

3 COURSEWORK: ENGLISH
A useful checklist

English

Speaking and listening: Your teacher will organise this for you, so you will not find anything about it in this section. Practise the advice given on page 59.

Examples of **Non-fiction writing** are an account of a visit to a concert, an outward bound expedition, writing based on work experience or a description of a protest march.

Examples of **Stories or other creative work** are a story set in the future, an autobiographical story or a selection of your best poems.

English literary heritage refers to the history of great English writers including those who have achieved fame since 1900.

You can take your set books into the exam to help you check facts and quotations. You may write in your books – but not long notes or essay plans.

You must comment on the ways at least one writer uses language and structure – and support your ideas by referring to the text. In this section your teacher will assess your writing to analyse, review and comment.

English Literature

If you choose a novel published after 1900 for the exam paper, you must study one published before 1900 for coursework – or the other way around.

- ▶ One of your pieces for **English Literature coursework** must be a **comparison** of one text with another – e.g. two poems.
- ▶ Another must show that you know something about the **social, cultural and/or historical background** to the text **or** how it fits into literary tradition. Your teacher will help you with this.

Your quick guide to the OCR English and English Literature coursework

English

A mark based on 3 selected speaking and listening activities  20%

Write to inform, explain and describe

Write to explore, imagine and entertain

 10%

A play by Shakespeare
A novel or short story/ies
Poems

 10%

Total = 40%

English Literature

Drama published before 1900 (can be Shakespeare)

A novel or short story/ies published before or after 1900 – depending on your choice of set books

Poems published before 1900

Total = 30%

You may use the same pieces for English and English Literature. Your teacher will tell you if they are suitable for both.

If you do, the total number of pieces you will have to do will be:

English writing = 2

English literary heritage = 3 = English Literature

Total = 5

COURSEWORK: ENGLISH

Writing for different purposes

OCR Coursework tests whether you can write for a variety of different purposes. They are listed below. You need to use a different style for each one.

These examples of **what the OCR examiners expect** are all taken from the Coursework marking instructions.

1 Writing to inform, explain, describe

Reason for writing: communicate facts and ideas clearly in an orderly way.

Examples: write accounts, respond to media material, make newspaper reports.

What the examiner expects

At Grade C — Communicate clearly and fully. Control and order explanations and begin to handle detail.

At Grade A — Use language which is consistently clear, accurate, helpful to the reader and confident.

2 Writing to explore, imagine, entertain

Reason for writing: create imaginative and original stories or poems; use language which will attract and excite the reader.

What the examiner expects

At Grade C — Write well-balanced stories with some explanation of interesting events, characters and backgrounds. Use language and structure for effect.

3 Writing to analyse, review, comment

Reason for writing: to comment critically on what you have read.

Example: a comparison of two poems commenting on the use of language. Part or all of your work in the English literary heritage will be used to assess this sort of writing.

What the examiner expects

At Grade C — Write intelligently at some length, extend some of the ideas and justify them in appropriate, secure language.

At Grade B — Begin to analyse and to write coherently, ordering ideas, using detail and technical language where necessary.

Three examples

Here are samples of three different sorts of writing from real folders.

▶ Match each one to one of the **purposes for writing** on page 40.
▶ Say how the style of each is **different** from the others.

A — SAMPLE ANSWER

Hardy sees nature as important and powerful, whilst man is small and insignificant alongside it. This is shown by the way in which Norcombe Hill is described as "indestructible" and the star, Sirius, is described as a "sovereign brilliancy". Man's insignificance is shown in the way that Hardy finds it hard to believe that something so powerful and majestic can be experienced by the "tiny human frame".

> **Tips**
>
> Notice the use of single/double word quotations built into a commentary. Compared with full length quotations, these save time and have a powerful effect when well used.

B — SAMPLE ANSWER

The glistening white dress floated down around my olive body. Its brilliant whiteness clashed with my dark skin. My hair fell around my face in soft midnight waves, and the comforting heat of the midday sun shone down brightly on my face.

> **Tips**
>
> Use adjectives and adverbs to create vivid pictures in this type of writing, but don't overdo it. What is added here by using *glistening, olive, comforting*?

C — SAMPLE ANSWER

The English language is constantly changing; for example, the language of William Shakespeare is different from that of Dickens and that of a modern television soap opera. It would be unimaginable (and to some incomprehensible) to hear a character in Brookside talking in Shakespearian language, or for Romeo to greet Juliet with, "Wotcha! Fancy coming for a quick pint then, luv?" The evolution of a language can be seen to be due to three main factors: foreign influences, changing attitudes and the technology of the day.

> **Tips**
>
> This sort of writing follows a train of thought. Make sure that each new sentence leads on from the one before and that no sentences are out of order.

COURSEWORK: ENGLISH

Drafting and redrafting

Four **Steps** to complete a coursework task:

STEP 4 Write the final draft

STEP 3 Discuss – then edit, revise and correct

STEP 2 Write a first draft

STEP 1 Create a plan

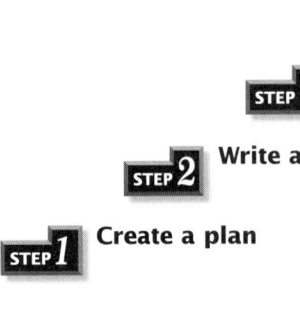

> **Tips**
> Work to deadlines for each step.
> Complete tasks quickly!
> Don't make unnecessary drafts.
> It's better to go on to the next assignment.

How to redraft

There are **two ways** to make a first draft better before you start to **correct**.

1 Edit

Editing is about words, how many there are and whether they are the right ones.

Checklist
- Are the words **correct**?
- Are they the **best** words?
- Are there too many words?
- Are there too few for the effect you want?
- Are the words in the right order?
- Have you repeated yourself?

2 Revise

This is when you make a major change to what you have written. Don't be afraid to rewrite a paragraph or section if it doesn't seem right to you.

Checklist
- Does the first paragraph make an impact? Is it relevant?
- Is any part unbalanced? i.e. too short or too long?
- Does the ending work or does it need changing?
- Are any sentences in the wrong order?

> **Activity**
> Suppose you had written this! Shorten it to under half its length.

Before you begin this test there are several things that you will find you need. You will need a pencil, inkpen, ballpoint or a felt tip pen, something to rub out mistakes such as an eraser, and a ruler or a straight edge – something you can measure millimetres with and draw a straight line.

Word processing

1 The OCR rules

You must handwrite **one** piece of your coursework. The rest may be word-processed/desk-top published.

2 Advantages

The final version looks professional, and you can:

- edit, revise and correct without crossing out
- move a sentence or a section to another part of your text
- work on a draft instead of having to write it out again.

3 Disadvantages

You have to know about spacing your work out and designing it.

The spellcheck can create problems. Be especially careful of the thesaurus – it can tempt you to use inappropriate words. Does it give UK or USA spellings? Don't be caught out!

You have to be a good proof reader – see section 4!

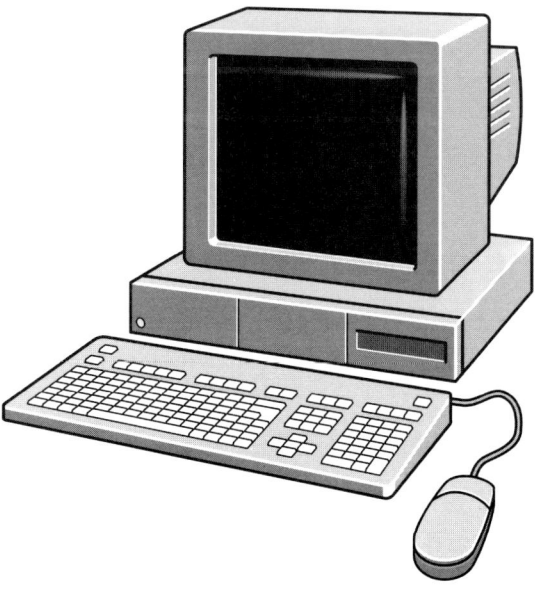

4 Proof reading

You may find you are more reliable if you use a paper copy and do not read from the screen.

Look for missing commas, letters missing from words, and letters in the wrong order.

A proof reading error will be counted as a mistake when your work is marked!

Activity

Correct this draft.

There is a mixture of 'natural' mistakes and mistakes made while word-processing. Why would this piece get a low mark?

```
A week before the car crash
me and my mum had to go to
may ausnties house in Newcastle
becuase my auntie and her
daughter had to go abroad
because she was goiung to get
her daughter married. In asian
weddingsd a week before two
freinds and relitives come
over come over to the house and
we have parties everynight so
that is why we had to go and
because she was my first cousin
anyway. They had packed all
of their lugage so they were
all set to go after a weelk.

Everything was going fine
everone was enjoying the
party my cousin came up to
me and said im getting married
in a weeks time everthing is
going great".
```

COURSEWORK: ENGLISH

How writers use language: useful tips

Writers choose words that best communicate their ideas. You have to find the links between the ideas and the choice of words. Learn to ask yourself questions like the ones on pages 44 and 45 to get a better mark.

Read the following poem by Tennyson.

1. Tennyson gives the impression of an eagle that is strong and tough. How do the words in line 1 give this impression?

The Eagle

He clasps the crag with crooked hands;
Close to the sun in lonely lands,
Ring'd with the azure world, he stands.

The wrinkled sea beneath him crawls;
He watches from his mountain walls,
And like a thunderbolt he falls.

3. Look at line 4. Faces are wrinkled and babies crawl! Why does Tennyson use these words about the sea – and what does it tell you about the eagle?

Tips
Say **clasps, crag, crooked** several times – then read the first line out loud.

2. Look at lines 2 and 3. What impressions of the eagle do they give?

4. Discuss the last line. Suppose Tennyson had written:

   And very quickly then he falls.

   What would he have lost?

Tips
Think: what do the **lonely lands** and the **azure world** mean to you?

How writers use language: useful tips

The Charge of the Light Brigade is one of the most famous of all war poems. As a result of a mistaken order, the British cavalry charged up a valley and were massacred by the Russian gunners stationed in the hills.

Here are two verses of the poem. You may be given the whole poem to study as part of your coursework.

The Charge of the Light Brigade

(iv)

Flash'd all their sabres bare,
Flash'd as they turn'd in air,
Sabring the gunners there,
Charging an army, while
All the world wonder'd:
Plunged in the battery-smoke
Right thro' the line they broke;
Cossack and Russian
Reel'd from the sabre-stroke
Shatter'd and sunder'd.
Then they rode back, but not,
Not the six hundred.

(v)

Cannon to the right of them,
Cannon to the left of them,
Cannon behind them
Volley'd and thunder'd;
Storm'd at with shot and shell,
While horse and hero fell,
They that had fought so well
Came thro' the jaws of Death
Back from the mouth of Hell,
All that was left of them,
Left of six hundred.

by Alfred, Lord Tennyson

1 What happens in these verses and how are they different?

2 How does the choice of words (including alliteration, repetition and rhyme) add to the detail of the battle and its extreme violence?

3 Read the two verses out loud. What do you notice about the rhythm of the poem? How does Tennyson create this rhythm?

4 COURSEWORK: ENGLISH LITERATURE

What the exam requires

One of your pieces must include reference to **social and historical influences and cultural contexts**.

This is about things that are important in the lives of characters in a book, but are different from the ways we live here and now. All the material you need will be in the book you are studying.

The passage on the right describes Oliver Twist's and Bill Sykes' walk through London on the way to committing a burglary. Read it now. Imagine the sights and sounds of London as Oliver would have experienced them. What are the differences between his journey and one that you would make today?

SAMPLE QUESTION

Describe some of the strongest influences on Oliver Twist's childhood and personality.

You should include the workhouse, Fagin and his gang, and life in London streets in the nineteenth century.

Although the task is about Oliver, all the things that are mentioned – the workhouse, gangland, and everyday conditions – belong to a bygone age and are social and historical influences and cultural contexts.

London rush hour

Nineteenth-century style

By the time they had turned into the Bethnal Green Road, the day had fairly begun to break. Many of the lamps were already extinguished; a few country waggons were slowly toiling on, towards London; now and then, a stage-coach, covered with mud, rattled briskly by: the driver bestowing, as he passed, an admonitary lash upon the heavy waggoner who, by keeping on the wrong side of the road, had endangered his arriving at the office a quarter of a minute after his time. The public houses, with gas-lights burning inside, were already open. By degrees, other shops began to be unclosed, and a few scattered people were met with. Then, came straggling groups of labourers going to their work; then, men and women with fish-baskets on their heads; donkey-carts laden with vegetables, chaise-carts filled with livestock or whole carcasses of meat; milk-women with pails; an unbroken concourse of people, trudging out with various supplies to the eastern suburbs of the town. As they approached the City, the noise and traffic gradually increased; when they threaded the streets between Shoreditch and Smithfield, it had swelled into a roar of sound and bustle. It was as light as it was likely to be, till night came on again, and the busy morning of half the London population had begun.

by Charles Dickens

Literary tradition

Literary tradition consists of writers and their works that form an important part of our heritage and the history of English Literature. For example, it is a literary tradition that **comedies** have been written by playwrights in Britain since the Middle Ages. In the eighteenth century, authors wrote **novels** that started a literary tradition leading to the books that we read today.

Sometimes a group of writers living at a particular time changed the way that literature was written. For example, the Romantic poets developed a new way of writing poetry in just a few years at the beginning of the nineteenth century.

Here are some literary traditions that may interest you

Poetry

Love poetry   War poetry
        Nature poetry

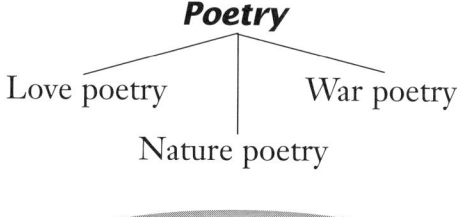

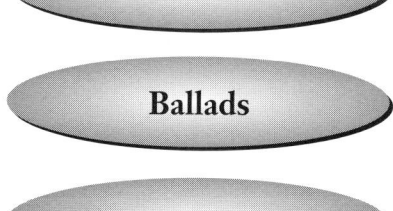

Narrative poems

Wordsworth	Byron	Shelley
	'Romantic' poets	
Keats	Coleridge	Tennyson

Donne	Marvell
'Metaphysical' poets	
	Herbert

Prose

'Gothic' writers; horror, mystery and detective stories in the 19th and 20th century.

Horror
Frankenstein
Dr Jekyll and Mr Hyde
Dracula
H G Wells

Mystery and suspense
Wilkie Collins
Dickens
Conan Doyle
M R James
Susan Hill
and other modern writers

Poetry, prose, drama

Tragedy

Women characters in literature

HOW TO TACKLE ENGLISH LITERATURE EXAM QUESTIONS

There are **three** different questions on every book you study for the exam.

You are asked to answer just **one**. This means that you have a fair chance to do your best on the day.

The first question is always set on a small section of your set book, which is printed on the exam paper. This is called a text-based question.

The other two choices are about different aspects of the set book. One might ask you to write imaginatively, for example as if you were a character from the book perhaps writing his or her diary.

Poetry: how to make comparisons – in six steps

Some questions ask you to choose poems from your selection that are on a particular subject and compare them. Others name – or print – two poems and ask you a question about them.

Read these poems about Autumn and then follow Steps *1* to *3* to a better grade.

I love the fitful gust that shakes
    The casement all the day,
And from the glossy elm tree takes
    The faded leaves away,
Twirling them by the window pane
With thousand others down the lane.

I love to see the shaking twig
    Dance till the shut of eve,
The sparrow on the cottage rig,
    Whose chirp would make believe
That Spring was just now flirting by
In Summer's lap with flowers to lie.

I love to see the cottage smoke
    Curl upwards through the trees,
The pigeons nestled round the cote
    On November days like these;
The cock upon the dunghill crowing,
The mill sails on the heath a-going.

The feathers from the raven's breast
    Falls on the stubble lea;
The acorns near the old crow's nest
    Drop pattering down the tree.
The grunting pigs, that want for all,
Scramble and hurry where they fall.

by John Clare

Gone are the lovers, under the bush
    Stretched at their ease;
    Gone the bees,
Tangling themselves in your hair as they rush
    On the line of your track,
    Leg-laden, back
    With a dip to their hive
    In a prepossessed dive.

Toadsmeat is mangy, frosted, and sere;
    Apples in grass
    Crunch as we pass,
And rot ere the men who make cyder appear.
    Couch-fires abound
    On fallows around,
    And shades far extend
    Like lives soon to end.

Spinning leaves join the remains shrunk and brown
    Of last year's display
    That lie wasting away,
On whose corpses they earlier as scorners gazed down
    From their aery green height:
    Now in the same plight
    They huddle; while yon
    A robin looks on.

by Thomas Hardy

Poetry: how to make comparisons – in six steps

 **Look closely at this question**

Question: *Compare the ways in which the choice of language, detail and the form in the poems tell us about the feelings of the writers.*

The question starts by referring to the **ways** the poems are written. The examiner doesn't want you to write about the choice of language and detail and form separately from the feelings of the writers, but to show how the two are linked.

Highlight **ways**, **language**, **detail**, **form**, **feelings**.

Form is the way the verses (stanzas) are written. Read the second poem aloud. You'll find that the short lines express the writer's feelings.

STEP 2 How to answer the question

▸ Give equal weight to each poem.
▸ Don't worry about the **right** answer. Explain yourself carefully and give examples from the poems. The examiner will credit you for your views.
▸ Underline or highlight any words or images you want to use in your answer; annotate the poems on the page if it will help.

 **Look closely at the wording of the poems**

1 Who's there in each poem?

2 What impressions do the details (like the curling smoke or the apples in the grass) give you?

3 What impressions do the words give? Choose the words that interest you most and highlight them.

4 The language and the verse forms are simple – but how do they illustrate the mood and feelings of the writers?

5 With all this evidence what have you worked out about the feelings of each writer?

Storm in the Black Forest

Now it is almost night, from the bronzey soft sky
jugfull after jugfull of pure white liquid fire, bright white
tipples over and spills down,
and is gone
and gold-bronze flutters beat through the thick upper air.

And as the electric liquid pours out, sometimes
a still brighter white snake wriggles among it, spilled
and tumbling wriggling down the sky:
and then the heavens cackle with uncouth sounds.

And the rain won't come, the rain refuses to come!

This is the electricity that man is supposed to have mastered
chained, subjugated to his own use!

supposed to!

by D H Lawrence

A thunder storm

The wind begun to rock the grass
With threatening tunes and low, –
He flung a menace at the earth,
A menace at the sky.

The leaves unhooked themselves from trees
And started all abroad;
The dust did scoop itself like hands
And throw away the road.

The wagons quickened on the streets,
The thunder hurried slow;
The lightning showed a yellow beak,
And then a livid claw.

The birds put up the bars to nests,
The cattle fled to barns;
There came one drop of giant rain,
And then, as if the hands

That held the dams had parted hold,
The waters wrecked the sky.
But overlooked my father's house,
Just quartering a tree.

by Emily Dickinson

Poetry: how to make comparisons – in six steps

STEP 4 — More helpful details for you to remember

An **image** says that something is what it isn't – and then leaves you to puzzle out why.
You know images as **similes** (A is like B) or **metaphors** (the same but without 'like').

Here are two riddles:

Lightning, says D H Lawrence, comes in jugfulls and tipples over and spills down. Impossible! You could never catch it!

Make the connection!
In your mind's eye you can see …

Emily Dickinson says that the lightning has a yellow beak and a livid claw. Impossible! Lightning isn't a bird of prey, and you don't see those shapes.

Make the connection! When lightning strikes the earth, you feel as if …

Which description of lightning do you prefer, and why?

STEP 5 — Answer this question and practise for a better grade

Question: *Compare the ways in which the writers use language and images to give us their impressions and thoughts about storms.*

STEP 6 — Ideas for revision

Work out carefully what the poems are saying to you.

- What pictures?
- What thoughts?
- What attitudes?

What should you do when you comment on details of language, imagery, alliteration, form and rhyming?

Choose the most suitable answer to the question:

A Find one example of each one and write it down.

B Write about all of them in a separate part of the essay.

C Keep it short: things like language are not important.

D Show how the way it is written helps us to understand the poem.

Answer: You should have chosen D. The others are wrong!

Extracts: how to tackle questions – in six steps

The first of the three questions on each book is always set on an extract.

Always find your answer to the question from the extract.

The first example is on a drama extract. All drama questions ask you to think of the play as if it is a performance.

Read the extract and then follow Steps 1 to 3 to a better grade.

Billy Liar

BARBARA Shall I go up, Mrs Fisher?

RITA (*imitating her*) Oooh, shall I go up, Mrs Fisher? If you can get up the stairs with them bow legs, you can.

ALICE It's all right, Barbara, I'll deal with this young madam. I've met her type before.

BILLY I think I can explain all this.

BARBARA Yes, I think you've got some explaining to do, Billy.

RITA He can explain until he's blue in the rotten face. It makes no difference to me.

ALICE If I knew your mother, young lady, wouldn't I have something to say to her.

RITA You can keep out of this. It's between me and him. (*To BILLY.*) Where's my ring? Has she got it? (*BARBARA'S right hand instinctively goes to her left.*) She has, hasn't she? You've given it to her, haven't you?

BILLY Ah, well – yes, but you see ... Only there's been a bit of a mix-up. You see, I thought Barbara had broken the engagement off.

BARBARA Billy!

RITA Yeh, well you've got another think coming if you think I'm as daft as she is. You gave that ring to me. And don't think you can go crawling out of it, 'cause you can't. You seem to forget I've got a witness, you know.

I've got two, 'cause Shirley Mitchem saw you giving it me, as well – so you needn't think she didn't. I can go down to the Town Hall, you know.

ALICE Now, don't come running in here with them tales, my girl. You know as well as I do he's under-age.

RITA Ask him if he was under-age down at Foley Bottoms last night. 'Cause I'm not carrying the can back for nobody. He wasn't under-age then. He was over-age more like.

ALICE Get out! Get out of my house!

BARBARA Have you been untrue to me, Billy? I've got to know.

RITA (*imitating her*) Oooh, have you been untrue to me, Billy! Get out of your push-chair, babyface. (*To BILLY*). You're just rotten, aren't you? You are – you're rotten all through. I've met some people in my time, but of all the lying, scheming ... anyway, you gave that ring to me.

BILLY Yes, but look, Rita ...

RITA (*interrupting*) Don't talk to me, you rotten get. Well, she can have you – if she knows what to do with you, which I very much doubt. You rotten lying get. Garr – you think you're somebody, don't you? But you're nobody. You miserable lying rotten stinking get.

BILLY Does this mean you're breaking off our engagement?

RITA You don't get out of it like that. I want that ring.

BARBARA	(*finding the right word at last*) Billy, have you been – having relations with this girl?
RITA	(*swinging round on BARBARA*) What do you think he's been doing? Knitting a pullover? You know what you can do, don't you? You can give me that ring. Because it's mine.
ALICE	If you don't stop it this minute! (To BILLY) As for you, I hope you know what you've done, because I don't.
RITA	Are you going to give me that ring?
BARBARA	I shall give the ring back to Billy – if and when I break off the engagement.
BILLY	(*moving towards her*) Barbara.
RITA	Yes, you can go to her. She can have you. And she knows what she can do, the squint-eye, bow-legged, spotty, snotty-nosed streak of nothing.
BARBARA	And you know what you can do as well. You can wash your mouth out with soap and water.
RITA	(imitating) Oooh, you can wash your mouth out with soap and water. You could do with some soap in your ears, you've got carrots growing out of them. Well, you can give me that ring. Before I come over there and get it.
ALICE	You can get out of this house. I won't tell you again.
RITA	Save your breath for blowing out candles. I want my ring. (*Crossing towards* BARBARA) Yes, and I'm going to get it.
ALICE	Get out of my house! Get out! Get out!

(GEOFFREY FISHER *emerges from the bedroom and comes slowly down the stairs.*)

RITA	(*moving right up to* BARBARA) Are you going to give me that ring, or aren't you?
GEOFFREY	(*half-way down the stairs*) Mother! ... Mother!
RITA	Because you'll be in Emergency Ward Ten if I don't get it – right sharpish.
BARBARA	Don't you threaten me.
RITA	I won't threaten you – I'll flatten you! Give me that cowing ring back! (S*he makes a grab for BARBARA'S hand.*)
BARBARA	(*pushing her away*) I won't ... I won't ...
ALICE	Will you stop it, the pair of you!
GEOFFREY	(*enters the room and stands in the doorway. He appears not to comprehend what is happening*) Mother!

(GEOFFREY'S *word silences* ALICE, BILLY, *and* BARBARA *who turn and look at him.*)

RITA	(*unconcerned*) Give me the ring!
GEOFFREY	You'd better come upstairs. Come now. I think she's dead.

THE CURTAIN FALLS.

by **Keith Waterhouse**

HOW TO TACKLE ENGLISH LITERATURE EXAM QUESTIONS

STEP 1 — Look closely at this question

Use this column to make your own notes for an answer to the question.

Question: *Explore the way the playwright makes the end of this Act dramatically effective.*

Highlight **dramatically effective**. It means that it 'grabs the audience's attention' or 'works well on stage'.

STEP 2 — How to answer the question

- Imagine watching and listening to the scene.
- Don't answer by going through the extract from beginning to end.
- This isn't a character question – but the way the characters behave is relevant.
- Find details to support all your ideas.

What the OCR examiners look for

- **What happens to the characters**: e.g. Billy's situation which is funny since he deserves it. But would you like to be in his shoes?
- **What the scene builds up to and why**: e.g. this scene gets more lively and is about to become violent when Geoffrey makes his shock entrance. Follow the reactions onstage to this.
- **Contrasts**: in this case what is funny and what is sad and shocking – the contrast is a dramatic effect.
- **Language**: e.g. Rita's rich language – very funny, but shocking and violent, and a lot of it. Also the way she mimics Barbara.

You now have four strong points to explain and to support with details from the extract.

Extracts: how to tackle questions – in six steps

STEP 3: Look at these quotations from sample answers.

See how these answers explain good points clearly and refer very closely to the text. The people who wrote them were all given Grade A when the complete answers were marked.

SAMPLE ANSWER 1

During the extract, Rita has arrived at the Fishers' household demanding her engagement ring. This part of the act is very dramatic, as beforehand Florence, the grandmother, has just been taken to bed and is very ill. This difference in itself is very dramatically effective.

Now, everyone is up in arms about the engagement ring, especially Rita. She imitates Barbara, e.g. "Ooh, shall I go up, Mrs Fisher?" and then insults her, e.g. "If you can get up the stairs with them bow legs, you can". The language Rita uses also helps the scene to be effective, e.g. "You rotten get" and "the squint-eye, bow-legged, spotty, snotty-nosed streak of nothing".

SAMPLE ANSWER 2

The ending also seems very active. Everyone is moving round a lot. This is shown by the stage direction "swinging round on Barbara". Most of the time it is Rita who makes the movements and they are nearly always to Barbara, "She makes a grab for Barbara's hand". This must be very effective. There is Rita going for Barbara, Alice shouting at everyone trying to stop them and Billy couldn't have been doing anything to stop them since he isn't mentioned at the end.

While all this is going on, no one notices or hears Geoffrey who has come down the stairs and is calling to Alice, because of all the shouting. Geoffrey again calls for Alice and this time everyone stops and turns to him, but Rita just carries on: (unconcerned: "Give me the ring").

SAMPLE ANSWER 3

We are laughing at what is a comic scene, with innocent Barbara fighting with loud-mouthed Rita. Rita swears and uses slang, while Barbara uses old fashioned words like "untrue", "having relations" and "wash your mouth out". It's a hilarious argument.

• • • • •

Geoffrey carries on regardless and says, "You'd better come upstairs. Come now. I think she's dead." He waits to the very last moment to deliver this shocking piece of news. It is totally unexpected by everybody, as previously Florence was a doddery old woman who talked to the sideboard, someone to laugh at.

The comedy comes to an end abruptly and the curtain falls. From now on the play has a more serious feel. Going from loud voices to silence in this scene prepares you for the change of direction.

Virtually all of the characters are on stage, so that we can see everyone's reactions. The stage will not be as full again in the play. This makes the scene feel even more important.

A tragic love affair

Parleyings were attempted through the keyhole, outside which she waited and listened. It was long before he would reply, and when he did it was to say sternly at her from within: 'I am ashamed of you! It will ruin me! A miserable boor! a churl! a clown! It will degrade me in the eyes of all the gentlemen of England!'

'Say no more – perhaps I am wrong! I will struggle against it!' she cried miserably.

Before Randolph left her that summer a letter arrived from Sam to inform her that he had been unexpectedly fortunate in obtaining the shop. He was in possession; it was the largest in the town, combining fruit with vegetables, and he thought it would form a home worthy even of her some day. Might he not run up to town to see her?

She met him by stealth, and said he must still wait for her final answer. The autumn dragged on, and when Randolph was home at Christmas for the holidays she broached the matter again. But the young man was inexorable.

It was dropped for months; renewed again; abandoned under his repugnance; again attempted; and thus the gentle creature reasoned and pleaded till four or five long years had passed. Then the faithful Sam revived his suit with some peremptoriness. Sophy's son, now an undergraduate, was down from Oxford one Easter, when she again opened the subject. As soon as he was ordained, she argued, he would have a home of his own, wherein she, with her bad grammar and her ignorance, would be an encumbrance to him. Better obliterate her as much as possible.

He showed a more manly anger now, but would not agree. She on her side was more persistent, and he had doubts whether she could be trusted in his absence. But by indignation and contempt for her taste he completely maintained his ascendancy; and finally taking her before a little cross and altar that he had erected in his bedroom for his private devotions, there bade her kneel and swear that she would not wed Samuel Hobson without his consent. 'I owe this to my father!' he said.

The poor woman swore, thinking he would soften as soon as he was ordained and in full swing of clerical work. But he did not. His education had by this time sufficiently ousted his humanity to keep him quite firm; though his mother might have led an idyllic life with her faithful fruiterer and greengrocer, and nobody have been anything the worse in the world.

Her lameness became more confirmed as time went on, and she seldom or never left the house in the long southern thoroughfare, where she seemed to be pining her heart away. 'Why mayn't I say to Sam that I'll marry him? Why mayn't I?' she would murmur plaintively to herself when nobody was near.

Some four years after this date a middle-aged man was standing at the door of the largest fruiterer's shop in Aldbrickham. He was the proprietor, but to-day, instead of his usual business attire, he wore a neat suit of black; and his window was partly shuttered. From the railway-station a funeral procession was seen approaching: it passed his door and went out of the town towards the village of Gaymead. The man, whose eyes were wet, held his hat in his hand as the vehicle moved by; while from the mourning coach a young smooth-shaven priest in a high waistcoat looked black as a cloud at the shop-keeper standing there.

by Thomas Hardy

 ## STEP 4 — More helpful details for you to remember

▶ Questions on novels and short stories include something about the way the characters live. In **text-based questions** the material you want is all in the text itself.

For example: Randolph's cruel behaviour to his mother was partly because of his education, his seniority in the family, his post as a priest and the way women were treated.

▶ When you answer the question in Step 5, be careful when giving your own feelings. It's easy to be angry, but bear in mind the social 'rules' of the time and Hardy's sympathy towards Sophy. Is Sophy a tragic character?

▶ When you write about Randolph, Sophy and Sam in your answer to the question below, **you don't have to write about them separately or in any particular order**. Plan your answer and check you have included everything in the question.

 ## STEP 5 — Answer this question and practise for a better grade

Question: *What are your feelings as you read this extract?*

You should consider:

▶ the behaviour of Randolph
▶ the behaviour of Sophy
▶ Sam's situation.

Try this question **even if you haven't read the story.** Sophy is a widow who has known Sam, a shopkeeper, for a long time and wants to marry him. Her son, Randolph, will not allow it because Sam's social class is not sufficiently 'respectable'. At the end of the extract, Sam sees Randolph going to Sophy's funeral.

 ## STEP 6 — Tips for revision

Use these tips to help you answer **drama** questions:

▶ the stage directions
▶ how characters react to each other and to what happens
▶ what happens when a different character comes on stage.

Use these tips to help you answer questions about **prose**:

▶ the houses people live in
▶ their manners
▶ their social class.

6 GENERAL REVISION

Tips to improve your reading

To improve your English, use this guide throughout the course, not just for revision.

- If you are a slow reader, try scanning groups of words rather than single words at a time. Don't struggle with reading that slows you down and is too difficult.
- You don't always have to read long pieces. In the exam, the passages will be quite short.

> **Tips**
> Read short passages twice.
> - Ask: what are the main points?
> - Study the details.
> - Do a mental check that you have understood.

Activity

- Plan regular, **varied** reading (not just sports pages or books by the same author).
- Keep a reading log of everything you read.
- Discuss it with your teacher.

What you should read

Find some reading time each week. Twenty minutes a day is a good start.

Try some of these:

Newspapers: A good local newspaper which discusses important issues and has interesting articles.

The Radio Times: Articles are lively, easy-to-read and are good for general knowledge.

Bestsellers and books of popular films: Good for up-to-date realistic stories.

Books and magazines about your special interests: Acquire specialist vocabulary by reading them.

Literature: Good readers should read a wide range of stories and novels including books published before 1900 (try nineteenth-century American short stories). Some simplified versions of longer books are worth reading.

Tips to improve your speaking and listening

Aim to be:

STEP 4 Clear and accurate when you explain something (like directions).

STEP 3 Entertaining – even amusing – when you tell a story.

STEP 2 Persuasive when you argue a case.

STEP 1 Courteous and fair to the people you talk to.

Tips

Expect to work in pairs, in small groups, or perhaps as a solo performer.

Beware! In pairs, don't let the other person do all the work. If you seem to be talking too much, use questions and comments to make your partner respond.

Beware! You are in a group where everyone interrupts and you can't be heard. Ask to move group – even if they are your friends.

How to improve your discussions with others

- prepare your thoughts
- explain your ideas
- take up others' comments
- summarise your own and others' ideas

- listen and speak courteously
- be prepared to change your mind
- don't mock others
- be sensitive to others' beliefs

- don't speak in single words
- speak clearly and audibly
- be enthusiastic
- remember eye contact and body language

Tips

When you lead a discussion, remember that control can change from one person to another. These hints will help you stay in charge of the proceedings.

- Introduce the topic clearly.
- Keep to task – but allow interesting digressions.
- Be firm with people who talk too much.
- Hurry the discussion along if it flags.
- Use 'open' (how? why? what?) questions rather than yes/no questions.
- Encourage everyone to take part.
- Be amusing, serious or challenging as appropriate.
- Don't talk too much, and remember – you can be wrong!

You can often choose a better word to explain what you want to say.

GENERAL REVISION

Tips to improve your writing

STEP 4 Show you know how to *build sentences*.

STEP 3 Show you know a wide range of *vocabulary*.

STEP 2 Get *punctuation* right.

STEP 1 Get *spelling* right

Improve your spelling

Most people should work hard at spelling. Mistakes are often the result of learning the wrong spellings when you were much younger.

Test yourself

DISAPPEAR   DISAPPOINTED
NECESSARY   SECRETARY
GOVERNMENT   ENVIRONMENT
TOMORROW   ACCOMMODATION
BEAUTIFUL   INDEPENDENT

If you can always spell these words correctly you are doing well.

Activity

1. Find the words you spell wrongly (from **all** of your written work).

   Good news! They are usually the same words over and over again.

2. Keep a list and learn the correct spellings like this:

3. Look at the word, say the word, cover it up and write it from memory.

Improve your punctuation

Common error number one: forgetting to end sentences with full stops.

A I opened the door cautiously, I immediately sensed that something was wrong, a moment later I was in the middle of a swirling mist. ✗

B I opened the door cautiously. I immediately sensed something was wrong. A moment later I was in the middle of a swirling mist. ✓?

C As I cautiously opened the door, I immediately sensed something was wrong. A moment later I was in the middle of a swirling mist. ✓

Common error number two: to forget to put , . and ? in dialogue. Remember, punctuation goes below as well as above.

"Look, over there," she said. "Don't you see it? It's the ghost of Coronation Street."

Tips

Make your dialogue interesting. Remember it should do a job like carrying events forward in a story or illustrating personality.

Tips to improve your writing

Increase your vocabulary

Activity

What's wrong with this?

I knew I was going to have a bad day when I got out of bed. I had thrown my clothes round the room the night before and when I got to the bathroom the water was cold and the heat was not on. I was very cold. It seemed much darker than the day before. I just did not know what was happening.

Answers

- too many short words
- few words that give precise meaning
- words like 'cold' and 'before' repeated

Try substituting words that have more meaning for everyday words, for example **bad** day becomes **miserable** and **thrown my clothes** becomes **scattered**.

Activity

I had wandered into the wood, trying to track down the location of the strange chirping sound that had fascinated me with its odd rhythms. Now I was aware that the pathway was narrower and that the holly bushes on either side were crowding in on me. Above me the tops of the tall pines were closer together and the sunlight no longer reached the undergrowth.

Why is:

- **Wandered** into the wood better that **walked**?
- **Fascinated** better than **interested**?
- **Holly bushes** better than just **bushes**?

Tips

Mix shorter and longer words. Use a long word where appropriate but not where a short word would be as good.

Never use a word with a general meaning when you can be more specific. Remember, **scarlet** is different from **red**.

How to join sentences

- Join strings of sentences with connected meanings.
- Don't be afraid of using **and** to join sentences, and don't overuse **but** and **so**.
- Practise joining sentences with **which** and **who**, **after**, **since** and **as**.
- Generally make sure that groups of sentences are well structured; but **short sentences mixed with longer ones** stand out well for effect.

Look back to page 60: **Improve your punctuation.**

Look at examples **B** and **C**.
Why is **C** better than **B**?

7 THE OCR EXAM!

Revision – the night before

Last-minute checklists

English checklists

- Check your records of spelling mistakes. (Separately? Believe? Parallel? Referee? Benefited?)
- Read the material you have been given for each paper. Remember you can't take your copies into the exam with you.

Non-fiction and media texts

- Think about the topic of the paper.
- Think out your views about the items in the material. They will help you with the writing question in Section B.

Literary texts

- Re-read the story: revise your views on the characters, events, settings, themes and language.
- Choose any book to read on the night before an English exam. New ideas and words can be useful the next day.

English Literature checklist

- Study your notes: you may remember the notes **you** make the best.
- Re-read your texts: poems need thoughtful and detailed reading even at this stage; skim-read the other texts, pausing at the parts you don't know so well as you thought.
- Pretend you have to give a talk on one of your texts and 'practise' it in your head.
- Remember to take your set texts with you!

Practical checklist

- Give yourself enough sleep the night before.
- Make sure you have two good pens that won't leak or run out – write in dark blue or black ink so that your work looks positive.
- Have something to eat and drink to give you 'exam energy'.
- Feel good and mentally prepared to accept a challenge.
- Get to school or college 15 minutes **before** you need to. Avoid panic!

The day itself – five steps to a better grade

STEP 5 *Check* what you have done.

STEP 4 *Time* yourself so as not to rush.

STEP 3 *Work methodically.*

STEP 2 *Plan* what to write.

STEP 1 *Read* the whole paper carefully.

STEP 1 Read the whole paper carefully

You have ten minutes reading and **thinking** time to:

- read the passages, once for gist and once for detail
- read the questions and start finding the answers
- start to think about what you will write.

You may need more than ten minutes to complete your preparation before you start to write.

STEP 2 Plan what to write

Use whatever sort of planning suits you best, like highlighting words on the question paper, making a formal plan with paragraph headings, making diagrams or writing a list of key words or quotations.

Know what you are going to write – including the ending – before you start.

STEP 3 Work methodically

Some people write from beginning to end, others write a paragraph and then stop to think.

- Think ahead so that you won't have to stop after each sentence.
- Work steadily so that your work does not look rushed.

STEP 4 Time yourself so as not to rush

Read any advice about timing and how long an answer should be. Give yourself time to do the last question properly.

STEP 5 Check what you have done

Look for:

- Anything that is carelessly phrased or doesn't make sense.
- Missing punctuation marks and capital letters.
- Spelling mistakes, especially simple ones like **across, all right, beginning, scared** and **giving**.
- Carelessnesses, like words missed out.

> **Tips**
> Don't be afraid of crossing out. The examiner won't mind if it is neat.

INDEX

Argument, writing an	21–23	Own words, using	9
Characters	33	Paragraphs, putting in order	23
Checking your work	37, 63	Personal writing	37
Commenting on content and style	14–20	Persuasive writing	20
Comparisons	48–51	Planning answers	22, 37, 63
Cultural contexts	46	Poetry questions	48–51
Drafting	42	Pre-released material	6, 7
Drama questions	52–55	Proofreading	43
Dramatic effectiveness	54–55	Prose questions	56
Editing writing	42	Punctuation	60
English coursework	39	Reading between lines	33
English syllabus	4	Reading: making it better	58
English Literature coursework	39	Reasons for writing	40
English Literature syllabus	4	Revising writing	42
Effects by writers	17	Revision	62
Highlighting words in questions	9, 49	Social influences	16
Historical influences	46	Speaking and listening	59
Images	44, 51	Spelling	60
Joining sentences	61	Story writing	37
Literary texts	24–37	Summaries	8–13
Literary tradition	47	Text-based questions	48–52
Media texts	6	Vocabulary	61
Non-fiction texts	6	Word processing	43
Notewriting	11, 22, 30	Words, writers' use of	15, 17, 44, 45, 48, 49
Other cultures	24–33	Writing coursework	40
		Writing: making it better	60